THE BEST OF

IRISH

COOKING

Tempting recipes for all occasions

EDITED BY ROSEMARY MOON

Gill & Macmillan

GRATEFUL ACKNOWLEDGEMENT IS MADE TO MR STEPHEN ODLUM
OF ODLUM GROUP LTD, DUBLIN, FOR PERMISSION TO REPRODUCE
RECIPES BY MAURA LAVERTY.

ILLUSTRATIONS BY CAMILLA SOPWITH
RECIPES SELECTED BY SARAH BOUNDS
INTRODUCED AND EDITED BY ROSEMARY MOON

CLB 4651
© 1996 CLB Publishing, Godalming, Surrey
Published in Ireland by Gill & Macmillan Ltd
Goldenbridge, Dublin 8
with associated companies throughout the world
Printed and bound in South Africa
ISBN 0 7171 2376 6

CONTENTS

INTRODUCTION

We know a great deal about the culinary traditions of Ireland because the Irish are a nation of story-tellers. Many sagas were recounted for hundreds of years before being written down for posterity, and I can only think of the Icelandic tradition of saga-telling as a rival to the Irish legends and folklore.

Until about 7,500 years ago Ireland was joined to the rest of the United Kingdom, but climatic conditions changed and the basin of what we now know as the Irish Sea flooded, leaving Ireland as an island of some 32,000 square miles off the west coast of England.

Remains of settlements from as long ago as 6,000 BC have been found in Ireland, along with bones, shells and husks that suggest the early peoples lived on a diet of wild boar and hare, salmon, trout, eel and sea bass, pigeon, duck and capercaillie, hazelnut and apple. Browse through the pages of this book and you will find that the basic diet has really changed very little – except that the caperciallie, a bird of the pine forests, is now extinct whereas it was once the common prey of huntsmen.

Stone-Age Settlers and Farmers

Around 6,000 years ago travellers from overseas settled in Ireland, although it is not exactly certain whether they came from Scotland, the north of England, Europe or even America.

The settlers started to clear some of the forests to make room for their crops and dwellings, growing wheat and barley and keeping cows and sheep. In time, these simple farmers were joined by a second group of settlers known as the 'passage grave builders', who were not only farmers but also builders in stone. Many clues to life in Neolithic times have been found in the extraordinary burial chambers that are to be found all over Ireland. The most magnificent of these is Newgrange, in the Boyne Valley, one of the oldest buildings in the world.

Clues to the prehistoric methods of cooking have been found at many of the early settlement sites, where stone troughs sunk into the ground are thought to have served almost as large saucepans; a fire was built by the pit, which had been filled with water, and stones were heated in the fire before being dropped into the water. Pieces of meat were then lowered into the hot water to cook. There is evidence of deep rock pools having been used in a similar way along the coast to cook fish.

Settlers, Invaders and Traders

A country as lush and verdant as Ireland has inevitably drawn settlers throughout history. The Celts arrived possibly as early as 500 BC and were certainly well settled by the first century AD. Around that time there was a climatic change, resulting in the type of weather conditions that we know today. This damp climate was ideal for growing oats, beloved of the Celts and still a popular ingredient in Ireland. However, despite good cereal crops of wheat, barley, oats and rye, the cornerstone of the economy remained the cow, and wealth was measured by the number of animals that an individual owned.

Young men tested and proved their manhood on cattle raids and these adventures provided plenty of material for the storytellers in each community. The greatest Irish saga tells the tale of the Cattle Raid of Cooley, and all sagas give valuable insight into life in these ancient communities.

Trade developed between communities and soon extended to overseas travellers from the continent of Europe. There are

records that as long ago as the 6th century the Irish were trading their wolfhounds for olive oil and wines from the Mediterranean. To this day Ireland enjoys a good political and commercial relationship with the rest of Europe and is a wholehearted member of the European Community.

St Patrick and the Early Christian Influence

The monastic communities that spread throughout Ireland following the evangelical work of St Patrick in the 5th century helped in the development of both the agricultural and culinary traditions of the country. Most of the communities were built behind walls, which not only protected and cloistered the monks from the outside world, but also provided shelter for their crops – Ireland can be a wild and windswept land for many months of the year. The monastic diet was fairly frugal, consisting mainly of grains, fruit and vegetables, but it was wholesome. Barley bread was eaten in the strictest communities. A rather wooden bread with little flavour, I would only recommend using barley mixed with other types of flour if a palatable loaf is to be achieved. The growing of oats, introduced by the Celts, was developed in the monasteries, and they soon became one of the principal crops – and oat bread the main variety for the majority of people.

Peas and Beans, New Foods from Normandy

When the Normans invaded Ireland in the 12th century they brought with them many new kinds of food, including peas, beans and globe artichokes. Peas and beans soon became valuable crops, playing an important part in the Irish diet. Eaten fresh, they were a new summer vegetable; left to go to seed and then dried, they provided a valuable food for the winter months.

The Normans also introduced rabbits and fallow deer, and began a tradition of keeping pigeons in elaborate houses similar to dovecotes. Pigeons are no longer especially kept for meat – they are natural scavengers and easy to shoot.

Although chickens, ducks and fish were common foods from earliest times in Ireland, the mainstays of the diet, right up to the 17th century, were oats and milk products. Meat was an occasional treat and although most families kept a pig for meat, the majority of meals were based on wild or cultivated vegetables, cereals and milk.

Cheese-making

The production of hand-made cheeses is an important area of growth in the Irish dairy industry today, but it is not a new industry. There are many references in Irish folklore and historical documents to the eating of curds, which was certainly one of the most important foods in the general Irish diet right up until the introduction of the potato. The curds were really one or two stages removed from pure cheese and were made by heating sour and sweet milk together until the curds formed. They had to be eaten very fresh as they still contained a vast amount of water, not having been pressed, but simply left to drain. Curds were said to be an excellent cure for such maladies as colds and stomach problems – they were quite bland and must have settled the stomach in much the same way as natural yogurt does today. Like other foods, curds became a form of currency, and just as a tenant might have paid his rent with a cow, so poorer farmers often paid their rent in curds.

The production of curds eventually began to give way to farmhouse cheese production – a pressed cheese, even one that has been only lightly pressed, has better keeping properties than curds, and cheese is generally salted, the salt acting as a preservative. Cheese as well as butter was made in most homes, especially in rural communities. Traditional cheeses included *tanach*, a hard cheese; a soft cheese made from heated sour milk curds, I imagine rather like an Edam or Gouda; *gruth*, a curd cheese made from buttermilk; and *milseán*, made from sweet milk curds and eaten as a dessert cheese at the end of a banquet or at harvest festival.

Death by Cheese

Cheese is frequently mentioned in Irish folklore, often in violent or devious contexts. The most famous warrior queen in Irish sagas, Queen Méabh of Connacht, is said to have been killed by a piece of tanach thrown by her nephew. It is also written that Hui Lilaig, a druid jealous of St Patrick's missionary successes, rode out to meet him with a curd cheese laced with poison. St Patrick didn't trust the druid, especially when bearing gifts, so he blessed the cheese, which turned into stones, exposing the druid's wicked intentions.

Most cheeses were made from cow's milk, but in poorer areas, where the farmers could not afford to keep cattle, both goat's and sheep's milk was used. Kilkenny was famed for its sheep's milk cheese, which was popular right up to the early years of the 19th century. In the last years of its production it is recorded that the cheeses, each weighing about 2lbs, were sold in Kilkenny market for a shilling each.

The Irish Cheese-making Revival

Many of the award-winning farmhouse cheeses being made in Ireland today do not follow traditional recipes. Cheese-makers from some of the major European cheese-producing countries – from France, Switzerland and Holland – have come to Ireland bringing with them a wealth of knowledge and experience, and the variety of cheeses being made here today reflects this new 'invasion'. What has drawn these artisans to Ireland are the superb pastures and the excellent quality of the milk that they yield.

In the summer of 1987 I bought a delicatessen which specialised in hand-made cheeses. At that time it was still difficult to purchase the new generation of Irish cheeses, but by the time I sold the shop four years later, we had been selling Mileens, Gubbeens, Gabriel and, perhaps my favourite of all, the delectably creamy Cashel Blue, with some success. All the cheeses were of superb quality.

Mileens is a creamy soft white cheese, very similar to a Camembert, and was really one of the first new cheeses in Ireland. Gubbeens is more like a washed rind cheese and has a uniquely pungent flavour that varies slightly at different times of the year. Gabriel is more like a Dutch or Swiss cheese, with a hard, firm texture similar to that of a mature Gouda, and a strong, biting flavour. Cashel Blue is a superb cheese that offers a serious challenge to the finest Stilton for a place on any cheese board. It is' creamy and mild, yet with a distinctive bite, but it must be handled with care if it is to retain its shape and texture. Cheddar-making was revived in Ireland on a commercial scale some sixty years ago, and this popular cheese has become an important part of the Irish dairy industry's successful export drive.

Butter-making and Buttermilk

Of course, any country that has a rich tradition of cheese-making will also be known for its butter, and that is definitely the case in Ireland. Certainly during the last century almost every cottage had the equipment necessary to churn butter, and the whole process was bound up with talk of fairies and countless superstitions.

The most common churn for butter-making, a *dash*, was made of oak or ash. It had a cover through which a long staff was put into the milk to agitate it until the butter rose to the surface of the churn. This might take an hour or more and was extremely hard work. The barrel churn, which is generally the one that I think of as the traditional butter churn, made butter-making an easier task but it was still hard work turning the churn by means of a crank.

Butter-making was often the work of the woman of the house and was done once a week, any surplus being sold at market. If the butter was to be eaten straight away it was left unsalted and was known as 'fresh' butter. Butter that was to be kept for a short while was salted, and any surplus that was to be stored for much later use was preserved with garlic and kept in sealed containers in the cold water of the local bogs.

The milk that was left, the buttermilk, was used either as a drink or for baking. Today, buttermilk is usually produced with a culture or enzyme and is much thicker than the traditional product. Until recently it was very hard to find in our modern supermarkets, but I am pleased to say that most large stores now seem to stock it.

Superstitions and Fairies

Despite their strong religious convictions, the Irish are a very superstitious people and there is much talk of 'Little People', 'Good People' or fairies, as well as of curses and spells inflicted by the devil and other evil spirits. It was formerly thought necessary to stay on the right side of the spirits if they were to be kept from interfering in such day-to-day activities as butter-making. What could be more exhausting or disheartening than to churn the butter for an hour or more only to find that there was no sign at all of the butter 'breaking', or separating out from the milk. Such a catastrophe was undoubtedly brought about by the evil spirits!

Everything had to be just right for butter-making. The type of wood used for the churn and other equipment had to be right, and often two or more woods had to be used. A twig from the rowan tree was often tied to the churn to counteract spells, while red rags would sometimes be tied to the tail of a cow after she had calved to keep the evil spirits away from her milk. If the butter refused to break after churning it was thought that a witch or an evil-eyed neighbour had 'overlooked' the cow and somehow spirited away the richness of her milk, thus preventing a fat content high enough for butter-making – there's nothing like a red rag round the tail to prevent such happenings!

Any visitors to a house at the time of butter-making were expected to take a turn at churning to bring good luck. It was inadvisable for a suitor of the daughter of the house to remove the butter from the churn, however, as such a task was more than likely to render him impotent – although ridicule from his peers was probably more to be feared.

Such stories may now be taken with a pinch of salt, but that in itself was added not only to preserve the butter but also to keep the evil spirits away as they were said to be frightened of salt. However, there were more gruesome tales surrounding butter-making – the milk was sometimes stirred with the hand of a dead man to keep the evil spirits away, and in some places the hand of a dead child was placed under the churn to achieve the same end. The strict health regulations which are the scourge of the present-day food industry were obviously not in force at the turn of the century as, unbelievably, these stories date from within living memory.

Crying over Spilt Milk

Milk was such a valuable foodstuff that great pains were taken not to spill it – if the milk was wasted there would be none until later that day or on the following day, when the cow was milked again.

If a cow kicked over the milking bucket it was said that the milk should be left for the fairies, who obviously needed it to have caused the cow to spill it in the first place. If crying or wailing was heard from an unknown and unseen child it was thought to be the fairies in need of the milk, so the first pail from the milking should be taken outside and gently kicked over, as if by accident, to appease the wailing. People were likely to observe such customs, as the accompanying tales of impending disaster if they didn't were intimidating – if the milk was not spilt it was quite likely that the cow would slip and break a leg, or worse, and a crippled cow would be an unthinkable disaster to a household that relied on its milk. Even in times of great hardship it was unimaginable that the family cow should be slaughtered for meat – it was far more important to keep her for milk, butter and cheese, as milk and cereals were the most important constituents of the Irish diet for so many centuries.

The Brehon Laws

The Brehon Laws are a remarkable code of conduct dictated by the Brehons, or Irish judges, and were formulated about 438 AD. The laws remained in place for centuries, and between the 8th and 13th centuries they were actually documented, which is how we know so much about them today.

According to these wide-ranging laws, land was the common property of the family and wealth was measured in cattle. One of the basic tenets of the laws was that the rich should share their good luck with those less fortunate than themselves. This was really the beginning of the legendary Irish hospitality, which is still so much in evidence today, although the laws are no longer part of everyday life.

It was compulsory to share your food and your home with any passing travellers, with no questions asked. Guesthouses and hostelries were obliged to keep a welcoming hearth and joints of meat on the boil in readiness for passing strangers. Cottages were built at crossroads to encourage travellers to stop and share the food of the family, and everyone would be welcome. Such a richness of spirit is hard to imagine in today's society, where everyone is concerned with attending to their own needs and those of their immediate family.

The Brehon Laws not only dictated that the Irish should be a hospitable people, but also gave strict instructions as to how food should be prepared. For example, they stated that bread made by a woman should be 'two fists in breadth and a fist in thickness', whilst a loaf made by a man should be twice as large – perhaps this was the origin of the different sizes of standard loaf tins that are in use today?

Hearths, Stoves and Wall Ovens

For many centuries all cooking was carried out over an open fire. Originally, meat and fish were cooked on sticks held over the flames, while breads were baked on hot stones. The stone troughs found at Ireland's ancient burial sites were the result of Bronze-Age culinary developments, but the real breakthrough came during the Iron-Age, when the first three-legged pots appeared. These were an ideal way of cooking as they were much smaller than the stone troughs and therefore could be heated more efficiently. They could be stood over a low fire or hot ashes and then left until the food in them, usually a soup, thin stew or a gruel, was cooked.

Such pots remained in use for many centuries, although small improvements were made over the years. The most significant of these was the bastaple oven, a covered pot that often had hot turfs placed on top of it to ensure an even heating. Bastaples were still in fairly common use at the turn of the century, while griddles, a flat iron skillet used for griddle cakes, potato cakes and many other Irish quick breads, are still in common use. Having mastered the art of baking with fairly rudimentary equipment, it is not surprising that the Irish have been reluctant to change their very successful baking techniques.

The fire itself was built directly on the hearth and not raised up in a basket or grate, which meant that it could be divided, allowing for the main pot to be stood over an intense fire whereas the bastaple could be placed over more gentle flames or hot ashes for baking, and a kettle could be kept warm by another small fire.

Of course, once chimneys were properly incorporated into most homes, a system of supports for hanging pots over the fire was developed. This did not come about until the 19th century, but it allowed slightly more sophisticated cooking techniques as it was possible to move the food further away from the fire, thus achieving a simmer for stews and a more gentle boil for steaming.

One of the earliest types of oven to be used in Ireland was the wall-oven, developed by monks in the medieval monasteries for the baking of bread. This they did daily in large quantities, in order to feed not only their own community but

16

the patients in the hospices and hostels that were attached to the monasteries. The ovens were made of brick and heated by lighting a fire, often of turfs and gorse twigs, on the floor of the oven to heat the cavity. Once the oven was up to the required temperature the fire would be swept out and the bread put in to bake.

There is still a wall-oven in daily use in Schull, County Cork, where Quinlan's Courtyard Bakery is reviving the traditional art of bread-making. The company has brought the master baker from the village, now in his eighties and with over forty years' experience in the art, out of retirement to help preserve the techniques of wall-oven baking. This has been a venture that has enjoyed wide publicity, with the baker and the bakery frequently featured on television and radio programmes reporting on the revival of interest in traditional Irish food.

Ranges were uncommon in all but the largest of farm and manor houses, and even there they were installed less than 100 years ago. Although traditional methods of cooking really changed very little over hundreds of years, there are, of course, many who now extol the virtues of the combination microwave oven for the baking of their daily soda bread.

A History of Brewing

The Irish have a great tradition of brewing. Mead and ale were popular drinks almost 2,000 years ago, and most people brewed up at home. Mead is made from honey, spring water, herbs and aromatics. Bees were widely kept as honey was the principal sweetener for all cooking and beverage-making. It was always important to have sufficient honey to make plenty of mead and bragget, a mixture of ale and honey fermented together. The rich and the poor all made their own drinks, and St Brigid, who might well be described as the patron saint of cooks and housewives, was renowned for the quality of her ale and mead. A redoubtable cook, it was a pleasure to dine and drink at her table and many reports are recorded of the excellence of her hospitality. St Brigid, however, was not the only saint that we know to have been fond of ale – St Patrick is reputed to have had his own brewer, whom he took with him on all his missionary journeys.

Early ales were made simply from malted grains, oats, wheat or barley, spring water and honey. Hops were not introduced for beer-making until the 16th century, and cider made from wild or crab apples was popular long before beer was common. Indeed, many Irish recipes today call for cider, reflecting the popularity of the drink.

The Heather Ale of Folklore

There are tales of a most magnificent brew, an ale flavoured by heather, that was beloved of the Vikings and much envied by the Irish. Having defeated the Vikings at the Battle of Clontarf in 1014, an Irish chieftain attempted to extract the recipe from a Viking prisoner who did eventually share the secret, having first watched the chieftain murder his son. However, the Viking then threw himself over the cliff, taking the chieftain with him, so the Irish never learnt the Viking secret. Of course, the Danes – the modern-day Vikings – retain a reputation for magnificent brewing to this day.

Anyone was free to brew their own ale in Ireland, but the Brehon Laws laid down strict guidelines for the selling of ale and the running of ale-houses. They stipulated how much could be drunk by the monks in their monasteries; even on feast days and holidays a tonsured monk was allowed only half as much ale as a member of the laity, despite being allowed the same amount of food.

The ancient ales and beers of Ireland have now given way to a world-famous tradition of brewing stout – a dark, creamy headed beer, the best-known of which is Guinness. Purists might argue that such a fine drink should not be used for cooking, but stout makes wonderful stews and casseroles, especially with beef, and is also an excellent flavouring for fruit cakes.

The Finest Whiskey in the World

The Irish gained an enviable reputation for the quality of their whiskey as early as the 15th century. Spirits are first thought to have been distilled in southern France, possibly in the 11th century, and were probably brought to Ireland by wine traders, the Irish importing large quantities of wines from France and Spain. However, it is likely that the first whiskey was distilled in Ireland by monks returning from sojourns in

France. Whiskey was first used for medicinal purposes, its warming effects bringing about a feeling of well-being in the sick.

Irish whiskey was originally flavoured with raisins and dates, so I would imagine that it must have been considerably sweeter than today's commercially produced spirits. Distillation on a large scale began in the late 17th century, but the whiskey lacked the richness and sweetness of that made in smaller quantities, so it was often mixed with water and fruits to make a punch.

Home brewing and distillation meant easy access to alcohol, which led to serious drink problems among the Irish, while smuggling was also commonplace, with wines and brandy being brought illegally into the country. Taxes were therefore introduced on the distillation of spirits in the 17th century in an attempt to curb excessive drinking. However, this merely served to encourage the illegal distillation of poteen.

Poteen, the Spirit of the Potato
One of the most famous of drinks in Ireland must surely be poteen, a spirit made from the distillation of malt, grain, potatoes, sugar, treacle, molasses and yeast. Always illegal, the distillation of this potent spirit has survived all attempts to suppress it. Travelling poteen makers, constantly hounded by excise men bent on catching the law-breakers and destroying their equipment, kept one step ahead of the law thanks to the help of their customers. The church, too, concerned by the effects of drunkenness on individuals and their families, frowned upon these illegal activities. Today, however, the clear liquid can still be bought by those with the right connections.

The Irish Potato
It is impossible to talk about Ireland and Irish cooking without mentioning the potato, and yet this humble tuber was not introduced until the closing years of the 16th century. It is not certain exactly how or when the potato arrived, but the most popular story is that it was first planted here by Sir Walter Raleigh. Another school of thought claims that potatoes were found on a ship that had been wrecked off the coast of Galway. However and whenever they arrived, there are records of them being grown in County Down in 1606.

The potato was quickly accepted by the Irish and within fifty years had become the staple food of a large part of the population. Forgotten was the diet of milk and cereals that had served the people so well for centuries; potatoes were the new food and it became accepted that the average Irishman could live well on 8-10lbs of potatoes a day, with a cup of milk at each meal and only very occasionally a meal of meat or fish. The potato required very little husbandry; once planted it needed to be earthed up, but could then be left, except for a little weeding, until ready to harvest. And this was not junk food, as so many easy diets today are. The potato provided sufficient vegetable protein, calories, vitamin C, iron and calcium to keep the Irish relatively healthy – it seemed an easy way of life.

The Great Famine

Such reliance on a single food was bound eventually to end in disaster, which struck in 1845 when potato blight caused the failure of the entire crop. Up until this time the potato had continued to gain in importance. As the population began rapidly to increase, more and more families were forced to rely on the vegetable for their survival. A shortage of suitable farming land, which precluded crop rotation, together with a disease that ravaged the potato crop for three successive years, led to the horrors of starvation and the tragedy of mass emigration.

After the failure of the harvest, great efforts were made to improve farming methods. Carrots, turnips and parsnips were grown more widely both to provide a crop and at the same time to put some goodness back into the land, while on larger farms fields were left fallow in order to regain fertility. Slowly, matters turned full circle. As more pastures became available there was a rise in the numbers of cattle and sheep grazed, and a subsequent upturn in milk production. The potato was definitely a permanent part of the Irish culinary scene, but it would never again be relied upon to provide the complete diet of the Irish people.

Life in the Big Houses

In the 18th and 19th centuries many house parties were held in the manor houses of Ireland, especially during the hunting season. Lavish banquets were served and the visitors were impressed by the excellent quality of Ireland's meat and agricultural produce. Many tender new vegetable and fruit varieties were introduced to Ireland by these wealthy landowners, who had experienced exotic fruits such as peaches in London and were determined to grow them for themselves at home. Since many of the houses had walled gardens and, latterly, conservatories, even plants as tender as the vine were introduced with a certain amount of success.

The Pleasure of Family Life

There are two things that stand out in my impressions of Irish life. One is the legendary hospitality of the people – not perhaps to the extent laid down by the Brehon Laws, but the real warmth of welcome that is extended to the visitor in this beautiful land. The second, and perhaps the most important, is the enormous value that is still placed upon the family unit in Ireland, and the importance of eating and drinking together and the sharing of everyday life. With such a wealth of marvellous produce to enjoy, long may this pride and companionship last.

Soups
&
Starters

Soup is the traditional way of beginning a meal in Ireland. Even today many Irish people will begin not one, but both meals of the day with soup, and some will eat soup in summer and winter. Traditional soups were a method of extracting every last bit of goodness from an animal carcass, the bones being boiled up to produce a stock, which was then flavoured with herbs and thickened with oatmeal or rolled oats. Such soups were often very thick and in the poorer households were served as the major part of the meal.

Wild Herb and Vegetable Seasonings
One of the most important 'herbs' used as a seasoning was the leek, which is still used extensively in Irish soups today. I refer to

it here as a herb as it has a very pungent flavour and a little goes a long way, thus it was often regarded as a 'pot herb', especially valuable for the flavouring of soups. Wild leeks grew freely in Ireland and these were picked to season many dishes. Leek skin is still used as a flavoursome wrapper for a freshly made bouquet garni, keeping all the herbs together so that they can easily be removed from the pot at the end of cooking.

Almost anything can be made into soup. All kinds of fruits and berries, wild leaves and cereals were put into the pot along with any tiny pieces of meat or fish that were available. I often wonder whether all soups must have tasted the same? This can so often happen in the modern kitchen, when similar ingredients and virtually identical seasonings are used without a recipe to produce a dish. However, I am certain that, as so much food would have been gathered from the hedgerows and fields, seasonal ingredients and flavourings would have made a pronounced difference to the resulting soups at different times of the year.

Seaweed Soups

Some very traditional Irish ingredients were used in soups. These included nettles and herbs such as wild garlic, and varieties of seaweeds gathered from the beaches. Dulse, laver and carrageen were almost certainly used in soups, and their popularity can be traced right back to the times of St Columba and the early church in Ireland.

When much of Ireland was starving after the failure of the 1847 potato crop, a soup kitchen was set up outside the Royal Barracks in Dublin by the chef of London's Reform Club. This was the model for the soup kitchens throughout the country, set up to relieve the effects of the famine. Wealthy Protestant landowners ran soup kitchens for the workers on their estates, many of whom were Roman Catholics. Thus anyone changing their religion at this time was called a 'souper', and the landowners were accused of using the soup in the cause of proselytism.

Starters

Starters are a relatively new concept in Ireland, having been introduced possibly as late as the beginning of this century.

Before this time, when a special meal or banquet was served, there may have been three courses, but each would have consisted of many dishes, rather like a running buffet. The first course of the buffet would certainly have included at least one type of soup as well as meat dishes and fruits.

Soup remains the most popular way to start a meal, and this is perhaps why the choice of Irish starters is still relatively limited. The art of potting meats, fish and cheese to preserve them for winter use has given rise to some splendid, pâté-like dishes that make excellent starters and may be quite heavily spiced.

The magnificent seafood of Ireland is now often used as the first course of a meal – what could be better than a cocktail of Dublin Bay prawns or a plate of huge, fresh oysters? The native oyster was more widely available in the 19th century and was to be found in great numbers on the west coast. However, the centre of the oyster industry today is Galway, where an annual festival is held in September to celebrate the importance of the oyster to the local economy.

Oyster farms are now producing top-quality Pacific oysters, which means that this king of moluscs is available fresh from Irish waters throughout the year – it was previously said that the native oyster should only be eaten when there is an 'r' in the month, from September to April. Happily, with the introduction of the Pacific oyster, this no longer applies.

FISH STOCK

Once you have perfected the simple art of making fish stock, you can create stunning fish soups. This is a very traditional recipe – you can use any white fish; oily fish such as herring and mackerel are not suitable. You may need to order the bones in advance from your fishmonger.

Makes about 850ml/1½ pints

INGREDIENTS
680g/1½lbs fish bones and
   trimmings
3 sprigs parsley
1 bay leaf
2 tbsps mushroom stalks or
   peelings
1 stick celery
1 small onion, roughly chopped
1 small carrot, roughly chopped
4 peppercorns
Small sprig lemon or common
   thyme
1.14 litres/2 pints water

Place all the ingredients together in a large pan and bring slowly to the boil. Skim off any scum, then simmer the stock, uncovered, for 20-30 minutes. Strain the stock through a large sieve lined with muslin and use as required.

VEGETABLE STOCK

A good vegetable stock is the base of so many traditional Irish vegetable dishes. In contemporary cookery, a well-flavoured vegetable stock is required for many vegetarian dishes.

Makes about 1.4 litres/2½ pints

INGREDIENTS
4 tbsps olive oil
2 onions, roughly chopped
2-3 leeks, thickly sliced
4 carrots, sliced
6 sticks celery, chopped
8 sprigs parsley
1 tbsp tomato purée
Salt and freshly ground black
   pepper
2 litres/3½ pints water

Heat the oil in a large pan, add the prepared vegetables and cook slowly for 2-3 minutes, without browning. Add the remaining ingredients and bring to the boil. Reduce the heat and simmer the stock for 1 hour, uncovered. Strain through a sieve and use as required.

CHICKEN STOCK

I find white chicken stock the most versatile for soups, and I always include the skin of the bird for maximum flavour. Remove any excess fat from the carcass before making the stock, as this will make it greasy.

Makes about 1.4 litres/2½ pints

INGREDIENTS
1 chicken carcass
2 large onions, roughly chopped
2 large carrots, sliced
2 sticks celery, sliced
Small bunch fresh parsley
12 black peppercorns
2 bay leaves
Salt
2 litres/3½ pints water

Place all the ingredients in a large pan and bring slowly to the boil. Skim off any scum that rises to the surface of the stock, then reduce the heat and simmer slowly, uncovered, for about 2 hours.

Cool the stock slightly and skim off any fat before straining through a sieve. Use as required.

CHICKEN CONSOMMÉ

*A consommé is a very light soup and a little fine
pasta is added to this recipe for texture. No stock should
be covered while it is simmering as it may become
cloudy – this is especially important with consommé, which
should always be crystal clear.*

Serves 4

Ingredients
1 chicken carcass, including
  giblets
1.4 litres/2½ pints water
1 medium onion, chopped
1 large carrot, sliced
2 sticks celery, chopped
Bouquet garni
60g/2oz vermicelli or fine
  spaghetti
Salt and freshly ground black
  pepper

Place the bones and giblets in a
large pan with the water, bring to
the boil, then simmer slowly,
uncovered, for 1 hour. Add the
vegetables and seasonings then
simmer for a further hour.

Skim any fat from the soup then
strain it into a clean pan and boil
rapidly until reduced to 850ml/
1½ pints. Stir in the pasta and
continue cooking for 5-10
minutes, until the pasta is cooked.
Season the consommé to taste
before serving.

IRISH BROTH

*The broth of this dish is traditionally served before the meat,
which then forms part of the main course of the meal.*

Serves 6

INGREDIENTS
900g/2lbs scrag end of lamb,
  trimmed
1.7 litres/3 pints water
90g/3oz pearl barley
Salt and freshly ground black
  pepper
1 onion, finely chopped
1 large carrot, sliced
1 small swede, diced
1 leek, sliced
2 sticks celery, chopped
Freshly chopped parsley to
  garnish

Bring the lamb and water to the boil in a large saucepan, then skim off any scum that forms. Stir in the pearl barley and seasonings, reduce the heat, cover and simmer for 1½ hours. Add the prepared vegetables to the pan, return to the boil, then continue to simmer gently for a further 1½ hours, occasionally skimming off any fat as it rises to the surface.

Remove the lamb from the pan using a slotted spoon and allow it to cool slightly. Take the meat from the bones, discarding them with any fat or gristle. Cut the meat into small pieces, return it to the pan and simmer for a further 20-30 minutes, until the meat is completely reheated. Season to taste and serve, garnished with chopped parsley.

VEGETABLE BROTH

A creamy soup of root vegetables, perfect for vegetarians or for serving before a main course of poultry or meat.

Serves 4-6

INGREDIENTS
1 large carrot
1 small turnip
1 medium potato
1 medium onion
1 small parsnip
570ml/1 pint milk
570ml/1 pint stock or water
Bouquet garni
6 peppercorns (tied in muslin)
60g/2oz flour
60g/2oz butter or margarine
Salt and freshly ground
   black pepper

Peel and roughly grate or finely chop the vegetables. Combine the milk and stock in a large pan, then add the vegetables, bouquet garni and peppercorns. Cover and simmer for 30 minutes, then remove the seasonings. Knead the flour into the butter and add the mixture to the soup, a little at a time, returning the soup to the boil after each addition, then simmer the soup for a further 5 minutes. Season to taste before serving.

YELLOW BROTH

This is a typical Irish vegetable soup thickened with porridge oats, although oatmeal can be used if preferred.

Serves 4-6

INGREDIENTS
1.14 litres/2 pints chicken stock
1 stick celery, chopped
1 medium onion, chopped
1 small carrot, sliced
Salt and freshly ground black
  pepper
60g/2oz butter or margarine
60g/2oz flour
30g/1oz rolled oats
120g/4oz chopped spinach
2 tbsps double cream
1 tbsp freshly chopped parsley

Add the chopped celery, onion and carrot to the stock in a large pan and season with salt and pepper. Bring to the boil, then simmer for 30 minutes.

Knead the butter and flour together then add the mixture to the stock, a little at a time, returning the soup to the boil after each addition. Add the rolled oats with the spinach and simmer for a further 15 minutes. Press the soup through a sieve, or blend until smooth in a liquidiser or food processor, then adjust the seasoning and stir in the cream. Garnish with the chopped parsley.

COUNTRY BROTH

This soup is really a meal in itself. Such soups are traditionally made with whatever is to hand, but this is a typical selection of ingredients for a substantial broth.

Serves 8-10

INGREDIENTS
1 onion
1 carrot
1 potato
7.5cm/3-inch piece cucumber
½ green pepper
2 tomatoes
5-6 lettuce leaves
2 sticks celery
2 tbsps oil
15g/½oz butter
90g/3oz macaroni
60g/2oz pearl barley
60g/2oz red lentils
1.7 litres/3 pints stock
1 tbsp freshly chopped mixed
  herbs or 1 tsp dried
Salt and freshly ground black
  pepper
1 small glass of sherry
2-3 tbsps single cream

Prepare all the vegetables and salad stuffs and chop them roughly. Heat the oil and butter in a large pan, then add the prepared vegetables, cover and sweat them slowly until soft but not browned. Add the pearl barley, macaroni and lentils, then stir in the stock and add the herbs and seasoning.

Bring the soup to the boil and simmer for 30 minutes. Season to taste, then mash the soup with a potato masher, or blend in a liquidiser or food processor until smooth. Return the soup to the pan, add the sherry and the cream and reheat gently before serving. The soup may be thinned down with a little milk or water if necessary.

MUSSEL SOUP

There are wonderful mussels to be found around the coast of Ireland – this soup is an excellent way of serving them.

Serves 6

INGREDIENTS

1.7 litres/3 pints mussels, bearded and scraped
1 onion, chopped
1 sprig parsley
150ml/¼ pint cider
60g/2oz butter
2 leeks, finely sliced
1 stalk celery, chopped
60g/2oz flour
1.14 litres/2 pints milk
Salt and freshly ground black pepper
¼ tsp freshly grated nutmeg
2 tbsps cream

Wash the mussels, discarding any that are open or broken. Place them in a large pan with the onion, parsley and cider, then cover the pan and place it over a moderate heat. Cook the mussels for 3-4 minutes, shaking the saucepan frequently. Remove from the heat as soon as the mussels open. Strain the mussels through a fine sieve, reserving the cooking liquor, then remove the mussels from their shells.

Cook the leeks and celery in the butter until soft but not browned, then add the flour and stir well. Gradually add the milk, seasonings and nutmeg, bring to the boil then simmer for 20 minutes. Press the mixture through a sieve, add the liquor from the mussels, the cream and the mussels, then gently reheat the soup before seasoning and serving.

SMOKED SALMON BISQUE

Irish salmon is, in my opinion, amongst the best in the world. This recipe sounds luxurious but if you make it with smoked salmon trimmings it is positively affordable. Most shops that slice their own salmon will happily give you the skin.

Serves 6

INGREDIENTS

Skin and trimmings from a side of
  smoked salmon, or 225g/8oz
  trimmings
1 onion
5-6 cloves
1 bay leaf
1 tsp salt
6 peppercorns
1 carrot, thickly sliced
1-2 sticks of celery, thickly sliced
60g/2oz butter
60g/2oz flour
1 tbsp tomato purée
1 glass dry white wine
Cream and freshly chopped
  parsley to garnish

Place the salmon skin and trimmings in a pan with the onion, stuck with 5-6 cloves, and the carrot and celery. Cover with cold water, add the seasonings and simmer for about 30 minutes. Remove the bay leaf from the pan.

Take the cloves out of the onion and return the onion to the pan. Remove the salmon skin with a slotted spoon and scrape off any remaining flesh, returning it to the pan. Strain half the liquid from the pan into a bowl and reserve it.

In another large pan melt the butter, stir in the flour and make a roux. Add the tomato purée and gradually beat in the strained stock. Bring to the boil, stirring all the time until it thickens, then add a glass of white wine.

Place the remaining stock, containing the fish and vegetables in a liquidiser or food processor, and blend to a thick paste. Stir this fish paste into the soup, season to taste and bring almost to boiling point. Garnish with a swirl of cream and chopped parsley before serving.

CREAM OF FISH SOUP

There is no fish in this economical, creamy soup – the flavour comes from a good home-made stock. Use white pepper, as black will overpower the taste of the fish.

Serves 4

INGREDIENTS
3 leeks, sliced
1 stick celery, chopped
60g/2oz butter
60g/2oz flour
850ml/1½ pints fish stock
Salt and white pepper
1 egg, beaten
2 tbsps double cream
Shrimps for garnish

Cook the leeks and celery in the butter for 5 minutes, but do not allow them to brown. Stir in the flour and gradually add the stock. Season lightly, then bring to the boil and simmer gently for 15 to 20 minutes. Add the beaten egg to a little of the hot soup, return it to the pan and cook for a further 2 minutes, without boiling. Stir in the cream, season and serve garnished with a few shrimps.

34

COD CHOWDER

A chowder is a thick fish soup, usually containing bacon and potato. This cod chowder makes an excellent lunch or supper dish.

Serves 4

INGREDIENTS
460g/1lb cod fillet, skinned
340ml/12 fl oz cold water
2 rashers smoked back bacon
4 medium potatoes, peeled and
    sliced
1 onion, chopped
700ml/1¼ pints milk
30g/1oz butter or margarine
Salt and freshly ground black
    pepper

Place the fish in a saucepan with half the water and simmer for 6-8 minutes. Drain the fish, reserving the liquid, remove any bones, then return the fish to the stock.

Dice the bacon and cook it slowly in a large pan until all the fat is extracted. Add the potatoes, onion, and the remaining water, then cover and cook for 10 minutes. Add the fish and fish stock then simmer the chowder for 5 minutes.

Stir in the milk and reheat the chowder until almost boiling. Add the butter, stir until melted, then season to taste with salt and pepper before serving.

MUTTON BROTH

A traditional broth of mutton or lamb stock thickened with pearl barley and root vegetables. Cabbage is also included – it is a very good ingredient in soup.

Serves 4-6

INGREDIENTS

60g/2oz pearl barley (this may be soaked overnight but it is not essential)
1.14 litres/2 pints mutton or lamb stock
1 medium onion, finely sliced
1 carrot, finely chopped
1 turnip, finely chopped
1 leek, finely sliced
Heart of a small cabbage, finely shredded
60g/2oz butter or margarine
Bouquet garni
Salt and freshly ground black pepper

Simmer the barley in the stock while you prepare the vegetables. Melt the butter in a frying pan, add the vegetables and cook for 3 minutes, without browning. Add the vegetables to the stock with the bouquet garni and seasonings and simmer for 20-30 minutes, until the vegetables are tender. Remove the bouquet garni, season the broth to taste and serve immediately.

KIDNEY SOUP

This is my ideal winter walking soup – a flask of this revives even the most frozen fingers and aching feet.

Serves 6

INGREDIENTS
340g/12oz beef kidney, thinly
  sliced
225g/8oz lean beef, chopped
1 onion, finely chopped
1 turnip, chopped
1 carrot, chopped
3 sticks celery, chopped
2 tbsps seasoned flour
60g/2oz butter or margarine
1.14 litres/2 pints stock or water
Salt and freshly ground black
  pepper

Coat the kidney, beef and vegetables in the seasoned flour, then fry them slowly in the butter until it has all been absorbed. Stir in the stock or water and bring to the boil, then cover and simmer slowly for 45 minutes, or until the meat and vegetables are tender.

Remove some of the kidney with a slotted spoon, chop it finely and set aside for garnish. Rub the soup through a sieve, or blend until smooth in a liquidiser or food processor. Season the soup to taste, add the reserved garnish and reheat gently, if necessary, before serving.

POTATO SOUP

You can make potato soup with milk or water, but the flavour is much better when it is made in the traditional way, with a good home-made stock. I think that chicken or vegetable stock is best.

Serves 8

INGREDIENTS
60g/2oz butter
900g/2lbs potatoes, sliced
2 onions, sliced
1 small carrot, sliced
Bouquet garni
Salt and freshly ground black
   pepper
1.14 litres/2 pints stock
570ml/1 pint milk
Freshly chopped chives

Melt the butter in a large pan, add the prepared vegetables and cook slowly until they are soft, but not browned. Stir in the seasonings and stock and bring to the boil. Cover and simmer slowly for 30 minutes, until the vegetables are tender.

Press the soup through a sieve or blend until smooth in a liquidiser or food processor. Return the soup to the pan and add the milk, then heat gently until almost boiling. Season to taste and serve garnished with a few freshly chopped chives.

NETTLE SOUP

The monks in Ireland certainly ate nettle soup over a thousand years ago. Always choose young nettles for a sweet flavour.

Serves 6

INGREDIENTS
570ml/1 pint nettles
60g/2oz butter
30g/1oz medium oatmeal
850ml/1½ pints stock
280ml/½ pint milk
Salt and freshly ground black
  pepper

Wear gloves when you are collecting the nettles and only choose the young, bright green leaves. Remove any stalks and chop the leaves finely.

Melt the butter in a large pan, add the oatmeal and cook until golden brown. Remove the pan from the heat and gradually add the stock. Bring to the boil, then add the milk. When the soup is boiling again, add the chopped nettles and cook for 4-5 minutes. Season to taste before serving.

LEEK SOUP

A perfect Saturday lunch – leek soup, fresh bread and a wedge of Irish farmhouse cheese.

Serves 4-6

INGREDIENTS
4 rashers back bacon, rinded
30g/1oz butter
4 leeks, sliced
460g/1lb potatoes, diced
850ml/1½ pints vegetable stock
Salt and freshly ground black
    pepper
150ml/¼ pint single cream
1 small leek, thinly sliced, for
    garnish

Chop the bacon into small pieces. Melt the butter in a large pan, add the bacon and cook for 2-3 minutes. Add the leeks and cook for a further 5 minutes, until just softened, then stir in the potatoes, stock and seasoning and bring to the boil. Simmer for 45 minutes.

Blend the soup in a liquidiser or food processor until smooth. Return it to the pan, stir in the cream and reheat gently without boiling. Serve garnished with the raw sliced leek.

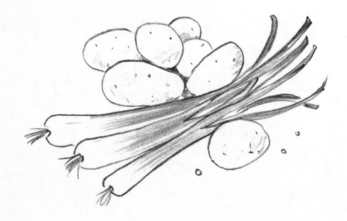

CREAM OF SPINACH SOUP

Spinach makes a vibrant green soup with a strong, peppery flavour – I sometimes add a little orange rind and juice, although this is not strictly traditional.

Serves 4-6

INGREDIENTS

1 small onion, finely chopped
60g/2oz butter or margarine
60g/2oz flour
Salt and freshly ground black
  pepper
460g/1lb spinach, finely chopped
570ml/1 pint stock
570ml/1 pint milk
Freshly grated nutmeg

Cook the onion in the butter until soft but not browned.

Stir in the flour, salt and pepper and cook gently until blended. Add the spinach with the stock and milk and bring briefly to the boil – do not overcook this soup or it will loose its vibrant green colour. Blend in a liquidiser or food processor until smooth.

Return the soup to the pan and heat gently but do not boil. Season to taste before serving, garnished with a little freshly grated nutmeg.

41

CREAM OF CARROT SOUP

Carrots make delicious soup, especially in the spring and summer when the young vegetables have a delicate, sweet flavour.

Serves 4

INGREDIENTS
1 tbsp oil
1 large onion, chopped
460g/1lb carrots, chopped
1 tbsp freshly chopped mixed
  herbs or 1 tsp dried
850ml/1½ pints chicken or
  vegetable stock
150ml/¼ pint soured cream
Salt and freshly ground black
  pepper

Heat the oil in a large pan then add the onion and cook until transparent but not browned. Stir in the carrots, herbs and stock and bring to the boil, then simmer for 30 minutes, until the carrots are tender. Allow the soup to cool slightly, then blend in a liquidiser or food processor until smooth.

Return the soup to the pan, add the soured cream and season to taste. Heat gently, stirring all the time, then serve.

CHICKEN LIVER PÂTÉ

Nothing from any animal was ever wasted by traditional Irish cooks. Chicken livers were made into pâtés to be served with soda bread or fresh toast.

Serves 4

INGREDIENTS
30g/1oz butter
1 small onion, finely chopped
Salt and freshly ground black
  pepper
225g/8oz chicken livers, trimmed
1 tsp Worcestershire sauce
60g/2oz butter, softened
1 tbsp brandy

Heat the butter in a frying pan, add the onion and cook gently until softened, but not coloured. Season well, then increase the heat and stir in the chicken livers. Cook them for about 2 minutes on each side, stirring continuously until just cooked through, then add the Worcestershire sauce.

Turn the contents of the frying pan into a liquidiser or food processor and blend for 30-60 seconds, until just smooth. Add the softened butter and the brandy and process again until the pâté is smooth. Transfer to one large dish or four individual serving dishes, and refrigerate until required.

DUBLIN BAY PRAWN COCKTAIL

Dublin Bay prawns are huge and delicious – use them for seafood cocktails on very special occasions. At other times it is more economical to use smaller prawns in the sauce, and then to garnish the cocktail with the Dublin Bay prawns.

Serves 4

INGREDIENTS
Cocktail sauce
4 tbsps mayonnaise
2 tbsps tomato purée
1 tsp Worcestershire sauce
2 tsps lemon juice
1 tbsp sherry
2 tbsps whipped cream
Salt to taste

5-6 lettuce leaves
225g/8oz cooked, shelled prawns
4 Dublin Bay prawns
Lemon wedges and parsley for garnish
Brown bread and butter for serving

Prepare the sauce by blending all the ingredients together and finally folding in the whipped cream. Season to taste then set aside.

Shred the lettuce leaves finely and arrange them in four glasses or dishes, then pile the prawns on top. Just before serving, top the prawns with the sauce and garnish with the Dublin Bay prawns, lemon and parsley. Serve with thinly sliced brown bread and butter.

WHITEBAIT

Bionn blás ar an mbeagán (the morsel is always tasty) is a proverb that was inspired by whitebait. I love whitebait and wish it was more widely used and appreciated.

Whitebait should be dry before it is cooked, or the tiny fish will stick together in clumps. Sprinkle with seasoned flour, then deep-fry until crisp and lightly browned – this will take about 3 minutes. Serve with lemon slices and brown bread and butter.

OYSTERS

It seems a pity to do anything to oysters – just serve them in their simple, natural splendour with lemon juice, pepper sauce and brown bread and butter. However, they are delicious dipped in seasoned flour, then in egg and breadcrumbs and deep-fried until golden-brown. Drain on absorbent kitchen paper and serve with lemon wedges and hot tartare sauce. Allow 6 oysters per person.

OYSTERS FLORENTINE

If oysters are plentiful and cheap, and especially if you are able to gather them yourself, you can afford to experiment with cooking them. This makes a luxurious lunch dish.

Serves 2

INGREDIENTS
340g/12oz fresh spinach
30g/1oz butter
Salt and freshly ground black
  pepper
12 oysters on the shell
2 tbsps double cream
30g/1oz strong Irish Cheddar
  cheese, finely grated

Wash the spinach thoroughly, remove any stalks and place it in a pan with the water that is clinging to the leaves. Cover and steam for about 2 minutes, until the spinach has wilted. Older leaves may take longer to cook. Drain the spinach in a colander, chopping it with a metal spoon.

Return the drained, chopped spinach to the pan, add the butter and season well. Arrange the spinach in two individual ovenproof serving dishes.

Remove the oysters from their shells and poach them in their own liquor for about 2 minutes – do not overcook or they will become tough. Arrange the oysters over the spinach, spoon the cream over and scatter with the grated cheese.

Cook under a hot grill until the cheese has melted, or bake in the top of a hot oven (200°C/400°F/ Gas Mark 6) for 5 minutes. Serve immediately.

SMOKED SALMON ROLLS
WITH PRAWNS

The flavour of this starter, when made with prime Irish ingredients, is sublime.

Serves 4

INGREDIENTS
2 tbsps mayonnaise
1 tbsp whipped cream
2 tsps tomato purée
Lemon juice, to taste
Salt and paprika
225g/8oz peeled prawns
8 slices of smoked salmon, about
  30g/1oz each
Salad leaves for garnish
Fresh soda bread and lemon
  wedges for serving

Mix together the mayonnaise, cream, tomato purée and lemon juice, season lightly then fold in the prawns. Divide the mixture between the 8 slices of smoked salmon and roll them up into cones.

Serve the salmon rolls arranged on a salad garnish on individual plates, with fresh soda bread and lemon wedges.

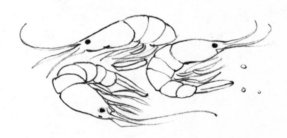

SMOKED MACKEREL PÂTÉ

*There are many excellent recipes for mackerel pâté –
this is one of the simplest, allowing the flavour of the
fish to dominate.*

Serves 4

INGREDIENTS
225g/8oz smoked mackerel fillets,
  skinned
90g/3oz butter, softened
Juice of 1 lemon
Freshly ground black pepper

Mash the mackerel fillets up in a
bowl with a fork, removing any
bones. Add the softened butter,
lemon juice and pepper and mix
thoroughly. Transfer to a serving
dish, or to individual ramekins,
and serve with wheaten soda
bread or wholemeal toast.

The pâté may be blended in a
liquidiser or food processor if you
prefer a smoother texture.

SMOKED MACKEREL PÂTÉ
IN ASPIC

*This sophisticated variation on a traditional favourite is
covered with a layer of aspic for presentation.
The aspic is home-made, but you could use a packet of
crystals if preferred.*

Serves 4

INGREDIENTS

225g/8oz smoked mackerel fillets,
  skinned and boned
60g/2oz butter, softened
Juice of ½ orange
1 tsp white wine vinegar
Salt and freshly ground black
  pepper
280ml/½ pint clear vegetable
  stock
2 tsps powdered gelatine
2 tbsps dry sherry
3 tbsps cold water

Place the mackerel, butter, orange
juice, vinegar and seasonings in a
bowl and mash them together
with a fork. Pile the pâté into a
serving dish and smooth the top.

Bring the stock to the boil in a
small saucepan, then remove it
from the heat and cool for 1
minute. Sprinkle the gelatine over
the stock, stir briefly and allow to
stand, stirring occasionally, until it
has completely dissolved – when
the gelatine has dissolved the
liquid should be clear. Add the
sherry and cold water.

Carefully spoon the aspic over the
top of the mackerel pâté, then
chill in the refrigerator until the
aspic has completely set. Serve
with fresh toast.

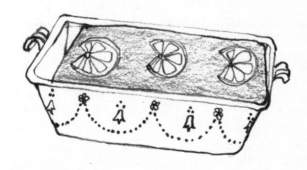

ANGELS ON HORSEBACK

These cocktail snacks may be made with canned oysters, but they are not the same as fresh, native oysters, which have a far superior flavour.

Makes 12

INGREDIENTS
Juice of 1 lemon
Pinch of salt
A few drops of Tabasco sauce
12 oysters, on the half shell
12 rashers streaky bacon, rinded
  and stretched

Combine the lemon juice, salt and Tabasco in a small bowl.

Remove the oysters from their shells and dip them in the lemon juice mixture. Wrap a rasher of bacon around each oyster and secure them with cocktail sticks.

Cook the 'angels' under a medium grill for 3-4 minutes, turning often, until the bacon is crisp. Serve by themselves or on warm fingers of toast.

IRISH RAREBIT

The secret ingredient of this is, of course, Guinness.

Makes 4 slices

INGREDIENTS
30g/1oz butter or margarine
30g/1oz flour
120ml/4 fl oz milk
1 tsp French mustard
1 tsp clear honey
120ml/4 fl oz Guinness
120g/4oz Irish Cheddar cheese,
 grated
Salt and freshly ground black
 pepper
4 thick slices freshly cooked
 wholewheat toast

Melt the butter in a heavy-based saucepan and stir in the flour to make a roux. Cook over a low heat for about 1 minute without allowing it to brown. Remove the pan from the heat and gradually add the milk. Bring slowly to the boil, stirring all the time, then stir in the mustard and honey and finally the Guinness.

Cook over a high heat for 2-3 minutes, then add the grated cheese and stir over a very low heat until all the cheese has melted.

Spread the mixture thickly on four slices of freshly cooked toast and brown under the grill.

STUFFED MUSHROOMS

Field mushrooms are one of my favourite vegetables for stuffing – they are so easy to deal with and they also have a magnificent flavour.

Serves 2

INGREDIENTS
4 freshly gathered field
   mushrooms
30g/1oz butter
1 small onion, finely chopped
60g/2oz fresh breadcrumbs
2 tsps freshly chopped chives
Salt and freshly ground black
   pepper
Freshly cooked toast or salad
   garnish for serving

Peel the mushrooms and remove the stalks. Chop the stalks finely, then cook them in the butter with the onion, until the onion is soft. Add all the remaining ingredients, mix well and use to fill the mushroom caps.

Cook the mushrooms slowly for about 5 minutes under the grill, until the topping is crisp and the mushrooms are cooked through.

If the mushrooms are very large you may need to grill them for a minute or two before stuffing them.

CREAMED MUSHROOMS ON TOAST

This dish is at its best when made with freshly gathered field mushrooms. When they are not available, use the large, cultivated variety.

Serves 4

INGREDIENTS
225g/8oz freshly gathered field
    mushrooms
570ml/1 pint milk
60g/2oz butter
60g/2oz flour
Salt and freshly ground black
    pepper
Freshly buttered toast for serving

Peel and slice the mushrooms, then place them in a pan with the milk. Bring slowly to the boil then simmer gently for ten minutes.

Meanwhile, melt the butter in another pan, add the flour to make a roux and cook slowly, without allowing the mixture to brown. Gradually strain the milk into the roux, stirring all the time, then bring to the boil. When the sauce has thickened add the mushrooms, season with salt and pepper and serve on buttered toast.

STUFFED VINE LEAVES

This might not sound like a traditional Irish recipe, but many country houses have vines growing either in conservatories or against sunny, south-facing walls.

Serves 8

INGREDIENTS
2-3 scallions or spring onions,
    finely chopped
2-3 tbsps oil
120g/4oz cold, cooked lamb,
    minced
225g/8oz cooked rice
1 tbsp freshly chopped marjoram
15g/½oz walnuts, finely chopped
Salt and freshly ground black
    pepper
24 vine leaves
280ml/½ pint stock
Lemon wedges for serving

Fry the scallions in the oil, then add the lamb, rice, herbs and walnuts and season with salt and pepper.

Have ready a pan of boiling water and a bowl of iced water. Hold the vine leaves by their stalks and dip each one into the boiling water for about 10 seconds, then plunge into the iced water. Lay the leaves, face down, on a board and place a teaspoon of the filling on each. Roll each one into a sausage shape, tucking in the edges, and gently squeeze into shape in the palm of your hand.

Pack the stuffed vine leaves into a large pan in one layer. Pour the stock over them and cover with a heatproof plate to keep them in position. Simmer for 30 minutes, then serve with wedges of lemon.

SPICED POTTED MEAT

This is a good way of using up left-over cooked meat and is a popular traditional dish in Ireland. Serve as a snack or a starter on fresh toast.

Serves 4

INGREDIENTS
460g/1lb cooked beef or pork
570ml/1 pint beef stock
¼ tsp cinnamon
¼ tsp nutmeg
¼ tsp ground ginger
1½ tsps thyme
1 tbsp Worcestershire sauce
Salt and freshly ground black
  pepper
Pinch of cayenne pepper
1 tbsp freshly chopped parsley
340g/12oz butter
Small bay leaves for garnish

Cut the meat into large cubes and place them in a pan with the stock. Bring to the boil, then cover and simmer for about 30-40 minutes, until the meat is tender and almost falling apart.

Drain the meat and mash it well with a fork. Beat in the spices, thyme, Worcestershire sauce, salt and pepper, cayenne and parsley, then spoon the mixture into small ramekins and chill.

Melt the butter in a saucepan over a low heat, then remove it from the heat and set aside until the solids sink to the bottom and the oil rises to the top. Pour the butter into a bowl through a sieve lined with a double thickness of fine muslin to remove the solids. Spoon a layer of clarified butter over the surface of the potted meat, then chill again until set. Garnish with bay leaves, then add a little more clarified butter to completely cover the meat. Chill until ready to serve.

DRISHEEN

This traditional white pudding is native to County Cork, and is often served fried for breakfast. You may have difficulty finding sheep's blood if you fancy making this at home – I'm afraid I can think of no alternative ingredient.

Serves 8

INGREDIENTS
1.14 litres/2 pints sheep's blood
2 tsps salt
570ml/1 pint full cream milk
Pinch of freshly chopped tansy or
   thyme
175ml/6oz fresh breadcrumbs

Strain the blood into a mixing bowl, add all the other ingredients and mix well. Leave to stand for 30 minutes.

Preheat the oven to 180°C/350°F/ Gas Mark 4. Pour the mixture into a greased ovenproof dish, cover with foil and place in a roasting tin with boiling water to come halfway up the sides of the dish. Bake in the preheated oven for 45 minutes, or until the drisheen is set.

Slice the drisheen when it is cold and fry it for breakfast.

VEGETABLES, SALADS & ACCOMPANIMENTS

It is almost impossible to think of Irish vegetable dishes without the ubiquitous potato springing instantly to mind. The potato was not, however, introduced into Ireland until the late 16th century so, although it may appear to be the most traditional of Irish vegetables, it is actually a relative newcomer.

Wild Leeks, Watercress and Tender Young Nettles
Vegetables that grow wild have been eaten in Ireland since prehistoric times. More recently, the best-known and most widely used of the wild plants were wild leeks, watercress, sorrel and tender young nettles. Some plants, such as wild onions, grew only in sandy soils so appeared in local dishes. Modern methods of cultivation now mean that they are grown and used extensively throughout Ireland. Other plants, such as orach and

goosefoot, both of which are similar to spinach in appearance and flavour, have completely disappeared from the culinary repertoire – both were boiled and mashed into a pulp, then served with butter.

Peas and beans have been used in Irish cooking from much earlier times than potatoes – they were introduced by French monks, probably around the time of the Norman invasion. Considered by many to be luxurious vegetables (in the same way that mangetouts and sugar peas still attract a premium price today) peas and beans were subject to tax as long ago as the 14th century.

Globe Artichokes from France

I suppose that I have only thought of globe artichokes as a fairly common vegetable for the last ten to fifteen years. As so many of the artichokes that are sold are still imported, I am constantly amazed to find that this vegetable has been known and enjoyed in Ireland for many years. Globe artichokes have been an important crop since Norman times – they grow so freely and well in Brittany and parts of Normandy that it must have been an obvious choice of vegetable for the monks to take to their new home in Ireland. What could be more mouthwatering than freshly cooked artichoke and creamy Irish farmhouse butter?

Another late arrival on Irish shores, although it is now one of the vegetables that springs immediately to mind when considering Irish cooking, is the cabbage. Native to Africa, it was brought to Ireland via Holland in the 16th century and has been a staple part of the Irish diet ever since. I always marvel at the sight of fields of large, firm cabbages – I find them, and cauliflowers, the most difficult of vegetables to grow at home.

Many great Irish houses have beautiful walled gardens and, being an island people, the Irish are well used to protecting their crops from the ravages of the weather. Especially in coastal areas, the tradition of walled gardens was essential to ensure that the crops grew well. These gardens were at their magnificent best in the 18th and 19th centuries, often producing marvellous crops of potatoes and cabbages, and it is easy to see why it is thought that these must always have been the country's main vegetable crops.

The walled gardens also led to experimentation with fruit and exotic plants – some, such as vines, had to be grown in glasshouses or conservatories, and in south-facing situations. They grew well in the days when each country house could afford a team of gardeners to tend to the produce.

Sea Vegetables for Variety

Ireland is famed for its use of the wild sea vegetables, or seaweeds, that grow freely around its coast. These plants are rich in sodium, iodine and magnesium and hence are a particularly healthy food. Carrageen, also known as Irish or sea moss, is generally used dried and is not actually eaten – it is boiled to extract a gelatinous paste that is often used to set milk puddings. I never feel that it actually tastes of anything, but it has a certain novelty value, especially at dinner parties!

Sloke and dulse are two other sea vegetables that are traditionally associated with Ireland, but my favourite is samphire – the seaweed that I cook most often. It looks like a tiny asparagus and has a vibrant green colour. Samphire grows on salt marshes and is not as common as the other seaweeds traditionally associated with Irish cooking. However, it may be found growing freely in sheltered, marshy coves on the east coast – a friend living in County Down gathers her own in mid to late summer. One of my favourite summer foods is a fresh salmon cutlet with pan-fried samphire and a rich buttery sauce – a perfect contemporary combination of the best of Irish ingredients.

COLCANNON

One of Ireland's most famous potato dishes, this is traditionally served at Halloween when it has charms hidden in the mixture – a ring for a bride, a bachelor's button, a sixpence for wealth and a thimble for a spinster.

Serves 4

INGREDIENTS
60g/2oz butter
120g/4oz onion, leek or scallion, finely chopped
460g/1lb cold mashed potato
60ml/2 fl oz full cream milk
Salt and freshly ground black pepper
225g/8oz cold cooked cabbage

Melt the butter in a large frying pan, add the onion and cook slowly until soft then add the potato and milk with the seasonings and stir over a medium heat until the mixture is warmed through.

Beat the cooked cabbage into the potato mixture over the heat – keep stirring and beating all the time until the mixture turns pale green and fluffy. Serve when heated through.

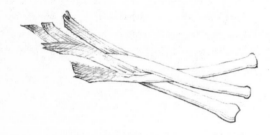

CHAMP

This is a traditional dish of the northern counties of Ireland. Forkfuls of the potato should be dipped into the melted butter in the top of each pile of champ.

Serves 4

INGREDIENTS
680g/1½lbs potatoes
120g/4 oz scallions or spring
   onions, trimmed and finely
   sliced
120ml/4 fl oz milk
 Salt and freshly ground black
   pepper
120g/4oz butter

Cut the potatoes into small pieces and cook them in boiling water for 20 minutes until tender. Drain well and keep warm until required.

Bring the sliced scallions to the boil in the milk and simmer gently until soft. Drain the scallions and beat them into the hot potatoes, gradually adding the milk to give a soft, fluffy mixture. Season well with salt and pepper then mound the potato onto four individual plates, making a dip in the top of each mound. Divide the butter between the four mounds of champ and allow it to melt before serving.

CODDLED POTATOES

*This is a potato dish that was traditionally served on
Saturday nights in Dublin.*

Serves 3-4

INGREDIENTS
680g/1½lbs small potatoes
120g/4oz streaky bacon, rinded
  and diced
2 large onions, finely sliced
1 tbsp freshly chopped parsley
Salt and freshly ground black
  pepper
570ml/1 pint vegetable stock or
  water

Peel the potatoes and slice them
thinly. Cook the bacon with the
onions in a large pan until the fat
runs from the bacon and the
onions are lightly browned. Add
the remaining ingredients, with
just enough stock to cover the
potatoes. Bring to the boil, then
cover and simmer slowly for 20
minutes, or until the potatoes are
cooked and tender. Serve
immediately.

HASHED POTATOES

*An excellent way to serve potatoes with sausages,
chops or burgers.*

Serves 4

INGREDIENTS
680g/1½lbs potatoes
2 onions, grated
Salt and freshly ground black
  pepper
45g/1½oz butter

Grate the potatoes then mix them
with the onion and season well.
Melt half the butter in a large
frying pan and press the potato

mixture into a thick cake in the
pan. Cook, covered, for 6-8
minutes over a medium heat until
the base is browned. Turn the
potato cake carefully onto a large
plate, then melt the remaining
butter in the pan. Gently slip the
potato cake back into the pan and
cook the second side until
browned. Serve immediately.

POTATO SCRAPPLE

This dish could be the inspiration for the modern snack food of crispy potato skins! It is a large potato patty which is cut during cooking to produce lots of crispy brown flakes of potato.

Serves 4

INGREDIENTS
460g/1lb cold mashed potato
460g/1lb cooked shredded
  cabbage
Salt and freshly ground black
  pepper
60ml/2 fl oz milk
45g/1½oz butter

Mix the potato and cabbage together and season well. Add sufficient milk to give a moist but not wet consistency.

Melt the butter in a large frying pan until it starts to brown, then add the potato and cabbage mixture, pressing it into a large patty. Fry for 3-4 minutes until the underside is browned, then turn it and chop it roughly with a knife, allowing the pieces of potato mixture to brown on both sides. The finished scrapple should consist of a collection of crispy, browned pieces of potato.

BAKED STUFFED POTATOES

*Baked potatoes are popular everywhere but very few
people really cook them properly. The Irish, with all their
history of potato growing, certainly know the best way to
cook perfect baked potatoes.*

Serves 6

INGREDIENTS
6 large potatoes for baking
30g/1oz butter
1 tbsp double cream
1 small onion, very finely chopped
1 tbsp freshly chopped parsley
Salt and freshly ground black
 pepper
120g/4oz Irish Cheddar, grated

Preheat an oven to 200°C/400°F/
Gas Mark 6. Scrub the potatoes,
prick them all over and bake them
in the preheated oven for 1-1½
hours until tender – the length of
cooking time will depend on the
size of the potatoes.

Cut a thin slice off the flat sides of
the potatoes and scoop out as
much of the potato as possible
without breaking the skins. Mash
the potato then mix it with the
remaining ingredients, except the
cheese, seasoning well with salt
and pepper. Pile the mixture back
into the potato skins and scatter
the cheese over the top. Return
the potatoes to the oven on a
baking sheet and cook for a
further 10-15 minutes, until the
cheese is melted and starting to
brown.

STEWED POTATOES

This is delicious served with sliced cold meats – it would also work well with pumpkin or squash.

Serves 4

INGREDIENTS
2 rashers green streaky bacon, rinded and chopped
1 onion, finely chopped
460g/1lb potatoes, cut into 1.25cm/½ inch dice
Salt and freshly ground black pepper
1 bay leaf
200ml/8 fl oz stock or water
1 tbsp freshly chopped parsley

Cook the bacon in a frying pan until the fat runs, then add the chopped onion and cook until lightly browned. Add the diced potatoes, season well and add the bay leaf and stock. Bring to the boil then simmer gently for 10-12 minutes until the potatoes are cooked but not mushy. Drain off any surplus liquid and serve garnished with the chopped parsley.

SCALLOPED POTATOES

Scalloped potatoes can be cooked in milk for everyday eating, but for special occasions I suggest that you use single cream.

Serves 4

INGREDIENTS
460g/1lb potatoes, sliced
1 onion, sliced
Salt and freshly ground black pepper
2 tbsps freshly chopped parsley
200ml/8 fl oz warm milk
60g/2oz Irish Cheddar, grated

Preheat an oven to 180°C/350°F/ Gas Mark 4. Layer the potatoes and onions in an ovenproof dish, seasoning well with salt and pepper and scattering chopped parsley over each layer. Finish with a layer of potatoes. Pour in the milk and scatter the cheese over the top. Cover and bake in the preheated oven for 1 hour, then remove the lid and cook for a further 20-30 minutes until the potatoes are crisp and golden.

POTATO SALAD

With such a tradition of potato growing and eating it is inevitable that the Irish should excel in the making of potato salads. The secret is to dress the potatoes while they are still hot.

Serves 4

INGREDIENTS
460g/1lb potatoes
2 tbsps vinaigrette dressing
2 tbsps mayonnaise
3 spring onions, finely sliced
Salt and freshly ground black
    pepper
1 tbsp freshly chopped parsley

Boil the potatoes in salted water for 15-20 minutes until just tender, then drain and dice them while still hot. Pour the vinaigrette dressing over the potatoes and leave until cold.

Carefully stir the mayonnaise, spring onions, seasonings and parsley into the potatoes – do not overmix or they will start to break up.

IRISH VEGETABLE SALAD

This is a mixed vegetable salad bound together with mayonnaise. Cut all the vegetables into small dice so that all the ingredients are roughly the same size.

Serves 4

INGREDIENTS
2 medium potatoes
1 large carrot
120g/4oz peas
120g/4oz French beans
175g/6oz cauliflower florets
1 tomato, seeded and diced
Salt and freshly ground black
    pepper
4-5 tbsps mayonnaise

Prepare all the vegetables and cut them into small dice. Simmer

them together, except the tomato, in boiling water for 5 minutes or until just tender. Drain and plunge immediately into cold water.

Shake the vegetables dry, then place them in a bowl with the tomato and season well with salt and pepper. Bind the salad together with mayonnaise and chill before serving.

STUFFED CABBAGE WITH ONION SAUCE

Cabbage leaves make a good alternative to vine leaves for stuffing, but it is essential to trim the stalk if you wish to roll the leaves. This recipe layers the stuffing with the blanched cabbage and is much easier to prepare than actually filling individual leaves.

Serves 4

INGREDIENTS
1 large cabbage
120g/4oz sliced bread
225g/8oz minced beef
225g/8oz sausagemeat
1 small onion, very finely chopped
Salt and freshly ground black
  pepper
1 egg, size 3, beaten

Onion sauce
2 medium onions, finely sliced
280ml/½ pint water from the
  cabbage
30g/1oz butter
30g/1oz flour
3 tbsps dried milk powder
Salt and freshly ground black
  pepper

Separate the leaves of the cabbage and discard the stalk, then cook the leaves for 5 minutes in boiling, salted water. Drain the cabbage well, reserving 280ml/½ pint of the water.

Soak the bread in a little stock or water for 2 minutes, then squeeze it dry and place in a bowl with the minced beef and sausagemeat. Mix well, then add the onion and seasonings and bind together with the beaten egg.

Grease a 1 litre/1¾ pint pudding basin then layer the cabbage leaves and meat mixture in it, starting and finishing with the cabbage. Cover with greased greaseproof paper and foil, tie securely in place, then steam gently for 1-1½ hours.

Prepare the onion sauce while the stuffed cabbage is cooking. Simmer the onions in the reserved cabbage water for 15 minutes or until tender. Add the butter, flour and milk powder and bring slowly to the boil, stirring constantly. Season to taste with salt and pepper.

Turn the cabbage out onto a warmed serving dish and serve sliced into portions with the onion sauce.

CABBAGE WITH TOMATOES & CHEESE

There is a time in early spring when cabbage seems to be just about the only green vegetable in season. This is a favourite way of making it more exciting.

Serves 4

INGREDIENTS

460g/1lb white or green cabbage, finely shredded
225g/8oz tomatoes, peeled and sliced or
200g/7oz can chopped tomatoes
Salt and freshly ground black pepper
1 tsp demerara sugar
90g/3oz fresh breadcrumbs
90g/3oz Irish Cheddar, grated
2 rashers streaky bacon, rinded and chopped

Preheat an oven to 160°C/325°F/Gas Mark 3. Cook the cabbage in boiling salted water for 5 minutes then drain it well, reserving 280ml/½ pint of the cooking water.

Mix the water with the tomatoes, seasonings and sugar and bring to the boil. Simmer the sauce for 10 minutes, or until the tomatoes are soft and the sauce has slightly reduced. Add a little extra salt and pepper if required.

Mix together the breadcrumbs and cheese. Butter an ovenproof gratin dish and layer the tomato sauce and cabbage in it, beginning with the sauce, and scattering each layer with a little of the breadcrumb mixture. Top the dish with the chopped bacon rashers then bake in the preheated oven for 30 minutes, or until the crumbs and bacon are browned.

SEA VEGETABLES

This is the 'in' term for a very traditional Irish food –
seaweed. Whilst it has been enjoyed for centuries
in Ireland and on other Atlantic coasts of the British Isles,
seaweed is only just finding its way onto the menus of top
cosmopolitan restaurants.

The three varieties of seaweed in common use in Ireland are dulse, sloke and carrageen.

Dulse

This is a reddish-brown seaweed often sold dried and which is usually eaten raw. It can be chewed, rather like tobacco. When gathering dulse from the rocks to use, it should be washed very thoroughly to remove all traces of sand and grit. It may be chopped very finely for adding to soups and casseroles but if it is to be served whole as a vegetable it requires a very long, slow cooking to tenderise it properly, and should be simmered in water or milk for 2-3 hours. Drain the dulse, then serve it with a knob of butter and plenty of black pepper.

Sloke

Sloke is found on the coasts all around Ireland and also in Wales, where it is known as laverbread. It is dark green in colour and is sometimes called sea-spinach as it looks very similar to spinach when cooked. Sloke should be cooked with very little water or it will become mushy. Wash the seaweed thoroughly then add it to a pan with just enough water in it to cover the surface – the water should be boiling. Return the mixture to the boil after adding the sloke, then cover the pan and simmer very slowly for 3-4 hours. Stir or shake the pan frequently to prevent the sloke from catching and add a little more water if necessary. Add salt and freshly ground black pepper before serving, and a little butter or cream. Some people like to add lemon juice or vinegar.

Sloke may be served as a vegetable and was traditionally eaten with mutton. It may also be made into patties or sloke cakes by mixing it with oatmeal, and these are delicious as part of a fried breakfast.

Carrageen

Carrageen is a moss-type seaweed, often known as Irish Moss. It is not actually served as a vegetable but is used as a setting agent for jellies and puddings and may also be used to thicken soups. Carrageen has to be boiled to extract the jelly-like setting agent and you should always be careful to scrape all the jelly from the underside of the sieve after cooking and straining the carrageen.

DULSE CHAMP

Dulse is one of the seaweeds that is native to Ireland and is reddish brown in colour with a strong flavour. It is usually eaten raw, but it can be made into a champ in place of scallions. Dulse requires long, slow cooking.

Serves 4

INGREDIENTS
120g/4oz dulse, soaked
Milk
680g/1½ lbs potatoes
Salt and freshly ground black
  pepper
120g/4oz butter

Soak the dulse for 3-4 hours in cold water, then rinse it thoroughly. Simmer the dulse for 2-3 hours, until tender, in sufficient milk to just cover, then drain it, reserving the milk. Cut the potatoes into small pieces and cook them in boiling water for 20 minutes until tender, then drain well.

Beat the dulse into the hot potatoes, gradually adding enough of the milk to give a soft, fluffy mixture. Season well with salt and pepper, then mound the potato onto four individual plates, making a dip in the top of each mound. Divide the butter between the four mounds of champ and allow it to melt before serving.

STUFFED MARROW

Marrows are a popular vegetable in Ireland. However, even in the Emerald Isle, they benefit from a well-seasoned, savoury stuffing.

Serves 4-6

INGREDIENTS
225g/8oz cooked lamb
1 onion
1 carrot
200g/7oz can chopped tomatoes
1-2 tbsps freshly chopped mixed
  herbs or
  1 tsp dried oregano
175-225g/6-8oz cooked rice
Salt and freshly ground black
  pepper
200ml/8 fl oz lamb or vegetable
  stock
1 large marrow
60g/2oz Irish Cheddar, grated

Preheat an oven to 200°C/400°F/ Gas Mark 6. Chop the lamb, onion and carrot very finely by hand or in a food processor, or mince them together. Add all the remaining ingredients except the cheese and mix well, adding as much stock as required to make a moist stuffing mixture.

Wash the marrow, cut it in half lengthways and scoop out the seeds. Place the halves in a buttered roasting tin and fill with the lamb and tomato mixture. Pour 1.25cm/½ inch of boiling water into the tin around the marrow, then cover the tin with foil. Bake in the preheated oven for 1 hour.

Remove the foil and check that the marrow is tender by piercing it with a sharp knife – if not, cook covered for a further 10-15 minutes. Remove the foil, scatter the cheese over the filling and return the marrow to the oven for 10 minutes, until the cheese has melted. Serve with salad and soda bread.

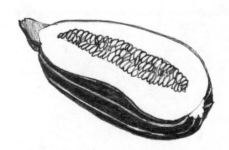

LENTIL LOAF

*Lentils, like all the peas and beans, were brought to Ireland
by the French. Combined with potatoes, they make a tasty
and inexpensive main course.*

Serves 4

INGREDIENTS
225g/8oz red lentils
30g/1oz butter
2 onions, chopped
570ml/1 pint vegetable stock
225g/8oz cold mashed potato
120g/4oz fresh breadcrumbs,
    white or wholemeal
1 tbsp freshly chopped parsley
Salt and freshly ground black
    pepper

Preheat an oven to 190°C/375°F/
Gas Mark 5. Rinse the lentils
under cold water in a sieve and
shake dry. Melt the butter in a
large pan, add the lentils and
onion and cook slowly for 5
minutes, until the onion is soft.
Add the stock and bring the

mixture to the boil, then cover
and simmer slowly for 20 minutes,
or until the lentils are tender. The
mixture should be dry when the
lentils are ready so avoid adding
extra water or stock unless
absolutely necessary.

Drain off any surplus stock from
the pan then add the potato,
breadcrumbs and seasonings and
mix well. Press the mixture into a
well-greased loaf tin, packing it
firmly so that the loaf will hold
together when cooked.

Bake for 30-40 minutes, until
golden brown. Turn out carefully
and serve sliced, with pickles or
chutney.

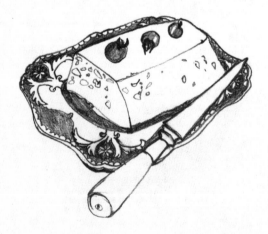

LEEKS AU GRATIN

*Leeks have always been popular in Ireland.
Originally they grew wild and were plentiful; although much
smaller than the modern, cultivated varieties, they had a
useful pungency to add to otherwise bland dishes. This is a
very popular way of serving leeks.*

Serves 4

INGREDIENTS
8 medium-sized leeks, trimmed
   and washed
45g/1½oz butter
45g/1½oz flour
280ml/½ pint milk
Salt and freshly ground black
   pepper
60g/2oz Irish Cheddar, grated
60g/2oz fresh breadcrumbs

Preheat an oven to 200°C/400°F/
Gas Mark 6. Wash the leeks
thoroughly to remove any dirt or
grit, then cut them into 2.5cm/1-
inch pieces. Cook in boiling,
salted water for 8-10 minutes then
drain, reserving 150ml/¼ pint of
the water.

Melt the butter in a pan, stir in the
flour and cook slowly for 1 minute
but do not allow the roux to
brown. Remove the pan from the
heat and gradually add the milk
and the reserved water from the
leeks. Bring slowly to the boil,
stirring all the time, then simmer
for 1-2 minutes, until thickened.
Add the grated cheese then
season the sauce to taste.

Arrange half the leeks in the
bottom of an ovenproof dish,
then cover with half the sauce.
Repeat the layers with the
remaining ingredients then cover
the dish with a layer of
breadcrumbs. Bake for 20 minutes
in the preheated oven, until the
breadcrumbs are browned and
crisp.

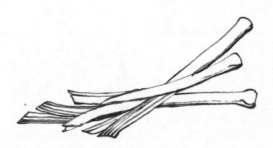

BUTTERED CARROTS

Carrots are used extensively in Irish cookery. This recipe is a celebration of the young vegetables – if you wish to use older carrots, peel and slice them, or cut into thick batons.

Serves 4

INGREDIENTS
460g/1lb young carrots, trimmed
45g/1½oz butter
Salt
1 tbsp freshly chopped parsley

Leave the carrots whole and place them in a pan with just enough water to cover. Bring to the boil then cover the pan and steam over a moderate heat for 10-12 minutes, until just cooked. The actual cooking time will depend on the size and age of the carrots.

Drain the carrots, return them to the pan and add the butter. Leave until the butter has melted, then season to taste with salt and add the parsley. Toss well and serve immediately.

BUTTERED JERUSALEM ARTICHOKES

These knobbly tubers deserve greater popularity as they have a delicious flavour, especially when lightly buttered and seasoned with wine vinegar. However, many gardeners despair of them – they are virtually impossible to get rid of once they have become established.

Serves 4

INGREDIENTS
680g/1½lbs Jerusalem artichokes, scrubbed
45g/1½oz butter
1-2 tsps white wine vinegar
1 tbsp freshly chopped parsley

Peel the artichokes carefully with a small, sharp knife, keeping the vegetable pieces as even-sized as possible. Bring a large pan of salted water to the boil, add the artichokes, then cover and simmer for about 15 minutes, until tender. Drain the artichokes and keep them warm.

Melt the butter, add the vinegar and parsley and mix well. Pour the mixture over the hot artichokes, then leave for a minute or so to allow the artichokes to absorb the butter before serving.

BRETONNE BEANS

Beans were among the many vegetables brought to Ireland by monks after the Norman invasion. Dried peas and beans soon became an important part of the diet, and this recipe for haricot beans is very much in the French tradition.

Serves 4

INGREDIENTS
225g/8oz haricot beans, soaked
  overnight

Stock
1 carrot, finely chopped
1 onion, finely chopped
1 tbsp freshly chopped mixed
  herbs

2 medium onions, finely chopped
30g/1oz butter
20g/¾oz flour
2 tsps tomato purée
Salt and freshly ground black
  pepper

Bring the beans to the boil in the water in which they have been soaking, then simmer for 40-50 minutes, until tender. Reserve 570ml/1 pint of the cooking liquor, and leave the beans in the remaining water until required.

Make the stock by adding the carrot and onion to the measured water with the chopped herbs. Simmer for 30 minutes, then reduce the liquid to 280ml/½ pint by rapidly boiling.

Cook the remaining onions in the butter in a separate pan over a medium heat until softened and browned. Stir in the flour and continue cooking until browned. Add the tomato purée, then gradually stir in the reduced stock. Bring to the boil, stirring constantly, then season to taste.

Reheat the beans if necessary, then drain them thoroughly and turn them into a warmed serving dish. Pour the sauce over the beans and serve immediately.

BUTTERED BEANS

Although this is a popular way of serving root vegetables such as carrots, it is a more unusual treatment for beans. However, the Irish have had to be inventive when fresh vegetables have been in short supply.

Serves 4

INGREDIENTS
225g/8oz haricot beans, soaked
  overnight
2 onions, finely sliced
60g/2oz butter
Salt and freshly ground black
  pepper
1 tbsp freshly chopped parsley

Drain and rinse the soaked beans, then place them in a pan with plenty of salted water. Add the onions and a knob of butter, then bring to the boil. Cover the pan and simmer the beans slowly for about 1-1½ hours, until very tender.

Drain the beans, then briefly return them to the pan over the heat to drive off any cooking liquid. Remove the pan from the heat and add the remaining butter, cut into small slivers, with salt and pepper to taste. Leave covered for 1-2 minutes to allow the beans to absorb the butter, then stir in the parsley and serve immediately.

PEASE PUDDING

Pease pudding is the traditional accompaniment to boiled bacon – a very popular Irish dish. Wrapping the split peas in muslin helps to produce a dry pudding – if you do not have any muslin, ensure that you drain the cooked peas very thoroughly.

Serves 4

INGREDIENTS
225g/8oz yellow split peas
1 tsp demerara sugar
Salt and freshly ground black
   pepper
30g/1oz butter
1 egg, size 3, beaten

Wrap the split peas in a large piece of muslin – do not wrap them tightly or they will have no room to swell during soaking. Leave to soak overnight in plenty of cold water.

Place the soaked peas in their muslin in a pan of fresh, salted water with the sugar. Bring to the boil then simmer for 30-40 minutes, until tender. Remove the peas in the cloth and drain them thoroughly - run the cloth under cold water until cool enough to handle, then squeeze the split peas dry.

Preheat an oven to 190°C/375°F/ Gas Mark 5. Remove the peas from the muslin then rub them through a sieve or blend them in a liquidiser or food processor until smooth. Season to taste then add the butter and beaten egg and pack the mixture into a buttered 570ml/1-pint ovenproof pie dish. Bake the pease pudding for 30 minutes, then serve with boiled bacon.

FRENCH BEANS WITH TOMATOES

This is a popular recipe for using up French or green beans towards the end of their season.

Serves 4

INGREDIENTS
60g/2oz butter
½ small onion, very finely chopped
225g/8oz ripe tomatoes, chopped
1 tbsp freshly chopped parsley
Salt and freshly ground black pepper
460g/1lb French beans, topped and tailed

Melt the butter in a small pan, add the onion and cook slowly until just beginning to soften. Stir in the tomatoes, parsley and seasonings, then simmer the sauce for 12-15 minutes, until the tomatoes are soft and the sauce has thickened.

Cook the beans in boiling, salted water for 8-10 minutes, then drain and turn them into a warmed serving dish. Season the sauce to taste and pour it over the beans to serve. The tomato mixture may be sieved to make a smooth sauce if preferred.

BOILED PARSNIPS

Parsnips are one of my favourite vegetables, but I very seldom boil them as they are usually rather large.

Serves 4

INGREDIENTS
8 small to medium parsnips
Salt and freshly ground black pepper
45g/1½oz butter
Lemon juice to taste

If the parsnips are really right for this recipe they will simply need topping, tailing and scrubbing.

Cook the whole parsnips in boiling, salted water for 15-20 minutes, until tender. Drain thoroughly, then return them to the pan and add the butter, cut into slivers, salt, pepper and lemon juice to taste. Cover the pan and leave for 1-2 minutes, shaking occasionally to coat the parsnips with the butter. Serve immediately.

PAN-BRAISED CHICORY

Chicory is not a very common vegetable in Ireland, but it is popular as a treat for special occasions. It is often eaten raw in salads. I actually prefer it cooked – it then loses much of its bitter flavour. This method of pan-braising is a quick way of cooking.

Serves 4

INGREDIENTS
4 medium heads chicory, trimmed
60g/2oz butter
4 tbsps stock
Juice of ½ lemon
Salt and freshly ground black
   pepper

Place the trimmed chicory heads in a single layer in the bottom of a saucepan – choose a pan that is only just large enough for them. Add the butter, cut into slivers, the stock and lemon juice, then season the vegetables lightly with salt and pepper. Cover the pan with a tight-fitting lid, bring to the boil, then simmer gently for 20 minutes until the chicory is just tender. Serve the chicory with the juices spooned over.

BRAISED CELERY

Celery is a very under-rated vegetable, but one that the Irish have always known how to use well in traditional dishes.

Serves 4

INGREDIENTS
1 head celery, trimmed and cut
    into 5cm/2-inch lengths
4 rashers streaky bacon, rinded
    and chopped
2 onions, sliced
1 carrot, thinly sliced
1 bouquet garni
Salt and freshly ground black
    pepper
280ml/½ pint vegetable stock
30g/1oz butter
15g/½oz flour

Preheat an oven to 200°C/400°F/
Gas Mark 6. Blanch the celery in a
pan of boiling water for 3-4
minutes, then plunge it into cold
water. Drain.

Mix the bacon, onions and carrot
together in a layer in the bottom
of an ovenproof casserole dish,
then add the bouquet garni.
Arrange the celery in a layer over
the vegetables, season lightly with
salt and pepper then pour the
stock over. Cover the casserole
with a tightly fitting lid and bake
in the preheated oven for 45-60
minutes, until the celery is tender.

Drain the stock into a pan and
keep the celery warm. Knead
together the butter and flour then
drop small amounts of the
mixture into the stock, stirring all
the time. Return the stock to the
boil after each inclusion and
season to taste when thickened.

Serve the celery very hot with the
sauce poured over.

ONION & TOMATO
CASSEROLE

*This is a simple Irish supper dish – serve with cold sliced
meat or just with freshly baked bread.*

Serves 3-4

INGREDIENTS
4 large onions
90g/3oz fresh wholemeal
  breadcrumbs
460g/1lb tomatoes, thickly sliced
Salt and freshly ground black
  pepper
60g/2oz butter

Peel the onions but leave them
whole. Place in a pan, cover with
cold, salted water and bring to the
boil, then simmer for 30 minutes.
Drain the onions and cut them
into quarters.

Preheat an oven to 190°C/375°F/
Gas Mark 5. Place 30g/1oz
breadcrumbs in the bottom of a
buttered, ovenproof gratin dish,
then add the onions and the
sliced tomatoes. Season well, then
top with the remaining
breadcrumbs. Dot with the butter,
cut into slivers, then bake in the
preheated oven for 35-40
minutes, until the breadcrumbs
are browned and crisp.

VEGETABLE HOT-POT

Some vegetables, such as leeks, garlic, parsnips and carrots are known to have been grown and eaten in Ireland since earliest times. Others, such as the famed Irish potato, are relatively new arrivals. Dishes such as this vegetable hot-pot have evolved from the thick vegetable soups so common in earlier times – were this to be boiled in sufficient water or stock it would make a very tasty soup. Baked in the oven, the vegetables retain their shape and texture and make a warming vegetable casserole.

Serves 4

INGREDIENTS

8 medium potatoes, sliced
1 head celery, trimmed and sliced
2 large onions, chopped
4 large carrots, thickly sliced
Salt and freshly ground black
  pepper
570ml/1 pint boiling vegetable
  stock, approx.
30g/1oz butter
Freshly chopped parsley to
  garnish

Preheat an oven to 180°C/350°F/ Gas Mark 4. Place the prepared vegetables in a buttered casserole dish, seasoning each layer well and ending with a layer of potato. Add sufficient boiling stock to just cover the vegetables, then cover with a tight-fitting lid and bake in the oven for about 1 hour, until the vegetables are tender. Much of the stock will be absorbed during cooking.

Dot the top of the hot-pot with slivers of butter and scatter with the parsley before serving.

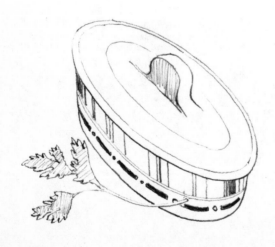

DRESSED CRAB SALAD

Think of Irish shellfish and you immediately think of cockles, mussels and oysters. Crab is also plentiful, and this is a contemporary recipe for an Irish crab salad.

Serves 4

INGREDIENTS
2 large cooked crabs
1 Iceberg lettuce
4 large tomatoes
4 hard-boiled eggs
16 black olives
280ml/½ pint mayonnaise
4 tbsps whipping cream
4 tbsps chilli sauce or tomato
  chutney
½ green pepper, seeded and
  finely chopped
3 spring onions, finely sliced
Salt and freshly ground black
  pepper

Prepare the crabs. Break off the claws then turn the crabs over and press up with the thumbs to separate the bodies from the shells. Cut the body into quarters and use a skewer to pick out the white meat. Discard the stomach sac and the lungs (dead man's fingers). Scrape out the brown meat from the shell. Crack the large claws and legs and remove the meat. Shred the meat, discarding any shell or cartilage, then combine all the crab meat and set it aside.

Shred the lettuce finely, quarter the tomatoes and chop the eggs. Combine the mayonnaise, cream, chilli sauce or chutney, green pepper and spring onions and mix well, seasoning to taste.

Divide the lettuce between four plates and arrange the crab meat on it. Spoon some of the dressing over each serving and garnish with the chopped hard-boiled egg, tomato and olives. Serve any remaining dressing separately.

HORSERADISH SAUCE

Horseradish grows freely in Ireland and is the traditional accompaniment to roast beef. The root has a fierce pungency and may well cause you to shed a tear or two whilst preparing the sauce, but take heart – the result is well worth the pain and anguish.

Serves 4-6

INGREDIENTS
15g/½oz butter
15g/½oz flour
150ml/¼ pint milk
2 tbsps freshly grated horseradish, squeezed dry
Good pinch of dry mustard
Salt and freshly ground black pepper
1 tbsp double cream (optional)

Melt the butter in a pan, stir in the flour and cook the roux over a low heat for a minute or so, without letting it brown. Remove the pan from the heat and gradually add the milk, then bring the sauce gently to the boil, stirring all the time. Use a very small pan for this small quantity of ingredients.

Stir in the horseradish and mustard, then season the sauce with salt and pepper. Add the cream, if used, then serve with roast beef.

PARSLEY SAUCE

This versatile sauce may be served with fish, vegetables or white meats. Use half milk and half wine for special occasions.

Makes 280ml/½ pint

INGREDIENTS
30g/1oz butter
30g/1oz flour
280ml/½ pint milk
Salt and freshly ground black pepper
2 tbsps freshly chopped parsley

Melt the butter in a pan, add the flour and stir gently over a low heat for 1 minute without browning. Remove the pan from the heat and gradually stir in the milk. Bring the sauce slowly to the boil, stirring constantly, then simmer for 1-2 minutes, until thickened.

Season the sauce to taste, then stir in the parsley just before serving – do not add it too long before serving the sauce or the parsley will lose its bright green colour.

CAPER SAUCE

This is an excellent sauce to serve with boiled bacon or gammon, although it was traditionally served with mutton.

Makes 570ml/1 pint

INGREDIENTS
60g/2oz butter
60g/2oz flour
280ml/½ pint milk
280ml/½ pint vegetable water
1 tbsp capers plus a little of their
    preserving liquid
Salt and freshly ground black
    pepper

Melt the butter in a pan, add the flour then cook the roux slowly for 1 minute without letting it brown. Remove the pan from the heat and gradually stir in the milk and vegetable water. Bring the sauce to the boil, stirring all the time, then simmer for 2-3 minutes, until thickened. Add the capers then season the sauce to taste with salt and pepper. Do not boil the sauce after adding the capers.

BREAD SAUCE

This is the traditional sauce to serve with roast chicken or turkey. The best bread sauce is always made with an onion stuck with cloves. To reheat the sauce, warm it gently over a pan of water – if heated directly it will become dry.

Makes 570ml/1 pint

INGREDIENTS
1 small onion
6-8 cloves
570ml/1 pint milk
60g/2oz fresh breadcrumbs
30g/1oz butter
Salt and freshly ground black
    pepper
1 tbsp cream

Peel the onion but leave it whole. Stick the cloves into the onion and simmer it in just enough water to cover for 15 minutes.

Strain off and discard the water, add the milk to the pan and simmer the onion in the milk for 5 minutes.

Strain the flavoured milk over the breadcrumbs then stir in the butter, cut into slivers, continuing to stir until the butter has melted. Season to taste, then stir in the cream just before serving.

FISH & SEAFOOD

Irish waters boast some wonderful fish; not only the sea but the lakes and rivers, too, yield a rich variety of fish, shellfish and edible plants. Several varieties are scarce in other parts of the British Isles; lamprey is plentiful in the waters of the river Shannon, while some inland lakes contain fish that appear only in summer and are not found elsewhere.

The Salmon, King of Irish Fish
The best-known of all Irish river fish, and the one most constantly referred to in folklore and legend, is the salmon. Irish salmon is amongst the best in the world, and although much is now farmed, it still manages to retain a good flavour. Traditionally, salmon was cooked whole for banquets and was often roasted over an open fire, having been basted with butter and honey. Strangely enough, it is only now that one or two companies are trying to market honeyed salmon – it may appear to be a new idea, but it is actually one of the most traditional of Irish seasonings for this king of fish. In the 18th and 19th

centuries salmon was also pickled, but this tradition appears to have died out.

A close relative of the salmon, the sea trout is plentiful around the west coast of Ireland during the early summer months. It is a heavenly fish, made sweeter by its very short season, and should be bought whenever the opportunity arises. Sea trout should be cooked simply and served with a spinach or sorrel sauce for a freshness and delicacy of flavour that is second to none.

Many Varieties of Trout

Ireland is able to boast several varieties of trout. Rainbow trout is usually farmed and there is a strangely unique variety, the red trout, that is sometimes caught in Blarney Lake and which is similar to char. While for many of us brown trout is a rare treat, this delicious fish is actually quite common in Ireland and benefits from simple cooking – I think pan-frying the fish wrapped in a rasher of bacon is the best method. Salmon trout is another name for sea trout.

Eel is still popular today and is a 'fish' that, in my opinion, benefits from smoking. Served as a starter with salad, smoked eel is quite delicious, although it is very rich and hence needs to be served in small portions. Young eels were traditionally boiled and then fried, but older fish were often finished in a white sauce. Today, the Irish eel fisheries are amongst the most important in Europe, rivalling those of Italy.

While Ireland is renowned for its deep-sea fish, such as cod, haddock and plaice, other varieties have played an even greater part in local history and folklore. Shark fishing was common on the west coast of Ireland, mainly for basking sharks which not only provided food for the fishermen but fuel for lights as well – one shark might yield up to 100 gallons of oil which fetched a high price for use in street lights in the major cities. It is no wonder that many fishermen were prepared to take great personal risks to hunt the shark. Shark fishing has now all but died out, killed by public opinion and alternative lighting fuels.

Herring – Food for Rich and Poor

One ancient industry that is still very much alive is herring fishing, although over-fishing has meant that this fish is no longer as common as it once was. Herring was a staple food of the poor in Ireland for many centuries and was often dried on large wooden racks on the beaches for winter use. They were also preserved by salting, and then smoked over turf fires. Today, thanks to modern distribution methods, herring is generally eaten fresh. Ideally, herring should be eaten on the day it is caught, which is why a fish eaten in a quayside café in a fishing village will always taste so much better than one bought at a fish counter miles from the coast.

The Irish Shellfish Tradition

Of course, very few people can think of Ireland without thinking of Molly Malone pushing her barrow loaded with live shellfish around Dublin's streets. While cockles and mussels will always be synonymous with Irish food, oysters, scallops, crabs and lobsters, not to mention limpets and sand eels, are also plentiful and of top quality.

For many years Ireland relied heavily on her fishing industry to feed her people, but today the catch is also exported widely, making an equally important contribution to the nation's balance of payments. Whether from the fish farms or from coastal waters, Ireland has earned an enviable reputation for the quality of her fish.

POACHED SALMON GARNI

A whole salmon, the centrepiece of so many Irish buffets, can look less than inviting after several portions have been removed. Divide the fish into pieces and it is will be much easier for your guests to help themselves.

Serves 8-10

INGREDIENTS
1 salmon, about 1.15kg/2½lbs
1 tbsp white wine vinegar
1 large lettuce
1 cucumber
5-6 hard-boiled eggs
3-4 firm, ripe tomatoes
2 lemons
Parsley to garnish
Mayonnaise for serving

Ask your fishmonger to fillet the salmon for you, leaving the skin on. Wrap each piece in buttered foil then lay the parcels in a pan just large enough to take them side by side. Cover with cold water, add the vinegar and bring slowly to the boil. Turn the parcels over carefully in the water, then remove the pan from the heat, cover and leave to cool.

Before the fish has cooled completely, unwrap the parcels and skin the fillets, removing any obvious bones at the same time. Divide the salmon into serving-sized pieces along the grain of the fish, then lay each piece in a nest made of a lettuce leaf.

Arrange the salmon nests in two rows on a serving platter, placing quarters of hard-boiled egg and pieces of lemon between them. Arrange two rows of alternating cucumber and tomato slices down the centre of the dish. Garnish with parsley and serve with mayonnaise.

BAKED SALMON

Baked salmon steaks are served here with a creamy spinach sauce – a perfect combination of traditional Irish ingredients.

Serves 4

INGREDIENTS
460g/1lb fresh spinach leaves,
  stalks removed
4 salmon steaks or cutlets
1 tbsp olive oil
1 tbsp lemon juice
30g/1oz butter
30g/1oz flour
280ml/½ pint scalded milk
1 tbsp freshly chopped parsley
Salt and freshly ground black
  pepper
1 egg yolk
1 tbsp double cream

Preheat an oven to 190°C/375°F/ Gas Mark 5. Wash the spinach thoroughly, then cook it in the water left clinging to the leaves in a covered pan for 3-4 minutes. Drain in a colander, chop thoroughly with a metal spoon, then blend the spinach to a smooth purée in a liquidiser or food processor.

Brush the salmon steaks with olive oil and lemon juice, then place them on a baking sheet and bake in the preheated oven for 20 minutes. Meanwhile, prepare the sauce. Melt the butter, add the flour and cook over a low heat for 1 minute without browning, then gradually add the scalded milk off the heat. Bring slowly to the boil, stirring all the time, then simmer for 1-2 minutes. Add the spinach purée with the seasonings and reheat gently. Blend a little of the sauce with the egg yolk, then add that to the pan with the cream. Reheat but do not boil.

Serve the salmon with the creamy spinach sauce spooned over.

BRAISED SALMON TROUT

Salmon or sea trout has a relatively short season, but is one of the most delicious of fish. If you see a salmon trout, buy it – the opportunities to buy this fish are few and far between.

Serves 4-6

INGREDIENTS
1 salmon trout, 900-1.15kg/2-2 ½lbs in weight
Salt and white pepper
1 small carrot, finely chopped
1 small onion, finely chopped
1 stick celery, finely sliced
75g/2½oz butter
Bouquet garni
150ml/¼ pint red wine
150ml/¼ pint water
15g/½oz flour

Preheat an oven to 190°C/375°F/ Gas Mark 5. Clean and scale the salmon trout; remove the fins and season the cavity lightly.

Cook the prepared vegetables in 60g/2oz of the butter until lightly browned – use a flameproof casserole dish large enough to take the trout, which may be curled round during cooking. Add the bouquet garni to the vegetables, then place the trout on top and pour the wine and water over. Cover the dish and bake for 35-40 minutes – the fish is cooked when the skin comes away easily from the thickest part of the flesh.

When cooked, remove the trout to a serving dish and return the casserole to the hob. Boil the cooking liquor rapidly until reduced by half. Knead the remaining butter and flour together, then add the mixture, a little at a time, to the reduced sauce, stirring constantly and boiling after each addition. Season to taste, then serve the sauce with the salmon trout.

STUFFED BAKED TROUT

There are several varieties of trout in Ireland: lake or brown
trout (often considered the finest), rainbow trout, salmon
trout and red trout. Any variety may be used for this recipe.
Use up to ¼ teaspoon of each type of pepper, depending on
how spicy you like your food.

Serves 4

INGREDIENTS
4 trout, about 225g/8oz each
120g/4oz butter
1 onion, finely chopped
2 sticks celery, finely sliced
1 small red pepper, seeded and
  finely chopped
4 spring onions, finely sliced
1 clove garlic, crushed
1 tbsp freshly chopped parsley
1 tsp freshly chopped dill
Pinch of white pepper
Pinch of cayenne pepper
Pinch of freshly ground black
  pepper
Pinch of salt
120g/4oz dried white or
  wholemeal breadcrumbs
2 eggs, size 3, beaten

Preheat an oven to 180°C/350°F/
Gas Mark 4. Clean the trout and
pat them dry. Melt half the butter
in a pan, add the prepared
vegetables and cook slowly until
soft, then add the herbs, the three
varieties of pepper and the salt.
Remove the pan from the heat,
mix in the breadcrumbs then
gradually add sufficient egg to
bind the stuffing together.

Stuff each trout with the
breadcrumb mixture, then place
the fish in a buttered, ovenproof
dish. Dot with the remaining
butter and bake, uncovered, for
about 25 minutes, basting
occasionally with any juices. The
trout may be browned under a
preheated grill after baking.

GRILLED TROUT WITH ALMONDS

*Every cuisine adapts recipes from other lands and makes
them its own – this classic trout recipe is as popular in
Ireland as it is elsewhere.*

Serves 4

INGREDIENTS
4 fresh trout
1 lemon, cut into wedges
60g/2oz butter
30g/1oz flaked almonds

Clean the trout and place a wedge
of lemon inside each one. Smear
the fish with butter then place
them in a foil-lined grill pan. Cook
under a preheated grill for 5-8
minutes each side, according to
size, then keep the fish warm on a
serving plate. Toss the almonds in
the butter remaining in the grill
pan, then brown them under the
grill. Scatter the almonds over the
fish and serve immediately,
garnished with lemon.

BAKED HAKE

*Irish hake is of very good quality – it is often caught by
Spanish fishermen who value it highly.*

Serves 4

INGREDIENTS
4 hake cutlets, weighing about
    175g/6oz each
Salt and white pepper
1 tsp lemon juice
Bouquet garni
150ml/¼ pint stock
150ml/¼ pint milk
2 tbsps fresh breadcrumbs
30g/1oz butter

Preheat an oven to 180°C/350°F/
Gas Mark 4. Place the cutlets in a
buttered dish with the seasonings,
then add the stock and milk.
Scatter the breadcrumbs over the
fish, dot the cutlets with butter
and bake for 30-40 minutes. Serve
the hake with the crumb topping
and a little of the cooking liquor
spooned over.

SOLE SURPRISE

An elegant way to serve fillets of lemon sole in a light pastry case.

Serves 4 as a starter

INGREDIENTS
225g/8oz prepared puff pastry
225g/8oz frozen chopped spinach
30g/1oz butter
4 medium fillets lemon sole,
   skinned
280ml/½ pint milk

Sauce
30g/1oz butter
30g/1oz flour
1 tsp freshly chopped fennel
60g/2oz Irish Cheddar, grated
Salt and white pepper

Preheat an oven to 220°C/425°F/
Gas Mark 7. Roll the pastry out
into a rectangle about 12.5x20cm/
5x8 inches, then cut into four.
Fold each piece over with the
short sides together, then cut out
the centres with a sharp knife,
leaving 1.25cm/½ inch all round.
Roll out the centre pieces until
they are the same size as the
boxes; damp them with a little
water, then place them under the
boxes to make firmer bases. Place
the pastries on a baking sheet and
brush with milk before baking for
10-15 minutes, until browned and
crisp.

Cook the spinach with 6mm/
¼ inch water and a little salt for 4-
5 minutes. Drain thoroughly in a
sieve or colander, pressing out as
much water as possible, then beat
in the butter. Poach the sole fillets
in the milk for 4-5 minutes,
depending on size, then remove
the fish and keep it warm.

Add the butter and flour for the
sauce to the warm milk and stir
continuously over a low heat until
the sauce has boiled and
thickened. Add the fennel and
cheese, then season with salt and
pepper.

Divide the spinach between the
pastry cases then top with a fillet
of sole. Spoon the cheese sauce
over and serve immediately.

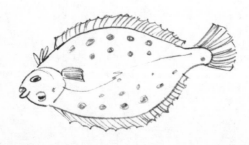

SOLE WITH CIDER SAUCE

Most of the sole caught off Ireland's shores is lemon sole.
Black sole, a much-prized delicacy that is simply brushed
with butter and grilled, is best served on the bone.

Serves 4

INGREDIENTS
680g/1½lbs lemon sole fillets
Paprika
150ml/¼ pint dry cider
30g/1oz butter
30g/1oz flour
Salt and white pepper
60g/2oz mushrooms, sliced
150ml/¼ pint single cream or full
  cream milk

Preheat an oven to 180°C/350°F/ Gas Mark 4. Place the sole fillets in a buttered dish, season lightly with paprika, then pour the cider over. Bake for 20 minutes, until the fish is just cooked, basting once or twice. Drain and reserve the cooking juices. Keep the fish hot.

Melt the butter, add the flour and cook the mixture over a low heat for 1 minute without browning. Gradually add the fish juices off the heat, together with the mushrooms. Bring the sauce slowly to the boil, stirring all the time, then add the seasoning and cream. Cook slowly until hot, but do not boil once the cream has been added.

Pour the sauce over the sole fillets and place the dish under a hot grill for 2-3 minutes, until the sauce bubbles and browns slightly. Serve immediately.

GRILLED PLAICE WITH
MAITRE D'HOTEL BUTTER

*Plaice is probably the most popular fish in Ireland – it is
relatively cheap and, up until now, has always been in
plentiful supply. Always choose plaice with bright spots,
which indicate the freshness of the fish.*

Serves 4

INGREDIENTS
4 medium plaice
2 tbsps lemon juice
Salt and white pepper
2 tbsps olive oil

Maître d'Hôtel butter
60g/2oz butter
1 tbsp freshly chopped parsley
Salt and white pepper
1 tsp lemon juice

Clean the fish, removing the
heads and black skin if preferred.
Slash the fish with a sharp knife,
season with lemon juice, salt and
pepper and leave for 20 minutes.
Prepare the butter by beating in
the parsley and seasonings. Shape
into four rounds then chill until
required.

Brush the plaice with the oil and
cook under a preheated grill for 5-
8 minutes on each side. Serve
with lemon wedges and the
seasoned butter.

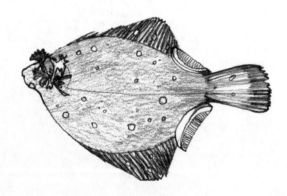

PLAICE & MUSHROOM TURNOVERS

Cooking plaice fillets in a puff pastry shell makes a filling lunch or supper dish.

Serves 4

INGREDIENTS
4 plaice fillets, skinned
Salt and white pepper
120ml/4 fl oz milk
120g/4oz button mushrooms, finely sliced
30g/1oz butter
Juice of 1 lemon
3 tbsps fresh breadcrumbs
340g/12oz prepared puff pastry
1 egg, beaten

Preheat an oven to 180°C/350°F/ Gas Mark 4. Season the plaice fillets lightly then roll them up and secure with wooden cocktail sticks. Place in a small ovenproof dish, add the milk and cook in the oven for 10 minutes. Drain the fish and allow it to cool. Raise the oven temperature to 200°C/400°F/ Gas Mark 6.

Cook the mushrooms with the butter and lemon juice for about 5 minutes, then cool slightly before stirring in the breadcrumbs. Roll the pastry out thinly and cut into four circles, 15cm/6 inches in diameter, then brush the edges with beaten egg.

Place a roll of fish in the centre of each pastry circle and top with a quarter of the mushroom mixture. Pinch the pastry edges together over the filling, enclosing it completely. Transfer to a greased baking sheet and brush with beaten egg. Bake the turnovers in the hot oven for 20-25 minutes, until the pastry is golden brown. Serve hot.

SKATE IN BLACK BUTTER

Skate has only been readily available in Ireland since fishing boats became larger and deep-sea fishing became more than a local industry. This is my favourite way of preparing it.

Serves 4

INGREDIENTS
4 small wings of skate
1 slice of onion
2 stalks parsley
Pinch of salt
6 black peppercorns

Black butter
60g/2oz butter
1 tbsp capers
2 tbsps white wine vinegar
1 tbsp freshly chopped parsley

Arrange the skate wings in a single layer in a large frying pan. Cover the fish with water and add the onion and seasonings, then bring slowly to the boil. Simmer the fish for 10-12 minutes, until just cooked through. Carefully remove the skate from the pan and remove the skin and any large bones – discard the water.

Melt the butter in a small pan and cook over a high heat until it begins to brown, then add the capers. Remove the pan from the heat and add the vinegar – this will cause the butter to bubble. Stir in the parsley and pour the sauce over the fish to serve.

SMOKED HADDOCK & EGG QUICHE

Smoked haddock and egg is a traditional Irish dish. This is a contemporary variation on the theme.

Serves 6

INGREDIENTS
175g/6oz fine wholemeal flour
Pinch of salt
90g/3oz butter
340g/12oz smoked haddock fillet
150ml/¼ pint stock or water
2 hard-boiled eggs, chopped
1 tbsp freshly chopped chives
90g/3oz Irish Cheddar, grated
3 eggs, size 3, beaten
280ml/½ pint milk
Salt and freshly ground black
  pepper

Preheat an oven to 190°C/375°F/ Gas Mark 5. Mix the flour and salt together, then rub in the butter until the mixture resembles fine breadcrumbs. Bind the pastry together with warm water, then roll it out on a floured surface and use to line a deep 20-22.5cm/8-9-inch flan tin. Prick the base with a fork and bake blind for 15 minutes.

Poach the fish in the stock or water for 8-10 minutes, then drain and flake, discarding any skin and bones. Mix the chopped eggs, chives and cheese into the fish, then spread the mixture over the base of the flan case. Beat the eggs and milk together and season lightly. Pour over the fish, then bake for a further 25-30 minutes, until set. Serve warm or cold.

KEDGEREE

Kedgeree was a popular breakfast dish in large country houses when entertaining on a lavish scale was common.

Serves 4

INGREDIENTS
460g/1lb smoked haddock
4 peppercorns
1 bay leaf
1 onion, finely chopped
60g/2oz butter
175g/6oz long-grain rice
½ tsp curry powder
1 tbsp lemon juice
Salt and freshly ground black
  pepper
1-2 tbsps freshly chopped parsley
4 hard-boiled eggs, quartered

Poach the haddock in a shallow pan of water with the peppercorns and bay leaf for about 10 minutes, until the fish is just cooked. Drain, reserving the cooking liquor, then bone and flake the fish.

Cook the onion in the butter in a large pan until soft, then stir in the rice and cook until transparent. Add the curry powder and cook for 1-2 minutes then add the reserved stock made up to 570ml/1 pint with water. Bring to the boil, stir, then cover and cook for 15-20 minutes, until the rice is cooked. Stir in the lemon juice, seasoning and haddock and heat gently, adding a little extra butter if necessary to keep the kedgeree moist.

Turn the kedgeree into a warmed serving dish and garnish with the parsley and hard-boiled eggs.

FRIED GOUJONS OF HADDOCK

Haddock, like plaice, is a very popular fish in Ireland. The breadcrumbs make a pleasant change from a batter coating.

Serves 4

INGREDIENTS
1 tbsp flour
1 tbsp freshly chopped parsley
Salt and white pepper
680g/1½lbs haddock fillets
1 egg, size 3, beaten
4 tbsps fresh breadcrumbs
Oil for deep-frying
Mashed potatoes for serving

Mix the flour with the parsley and seasonings. Cut the haddock into strips about 2.5cm/1 inch wide, then dip them into the flour, the egg and finally the breadcrumbs. Tie each piece into a knot, then deep-fry in oil preheated to 180°C/360°F until golden brown. Drain the fish on crumpled absorbent kitchen paper, then serve the goujons around a mound of mashed potato.

MACKEREL ROLLS

Fresh mackerel should ideally be cooked on the day that it is caught, but once cooked it will keep a day or two to make these tasty rolls.

Serves 4

INGREDIENTS
4 long, crusty rolls, or one French stick
1-2 tbsps roughly chopped walnuts
1 dessert apple, diced
½ tsp freshly chopped thyme
½ tsp freshly chopped mint
Salt and freshly ground black pepper
340g/12oz cooked mackerel fillets, skinned
4 tbsps natural yogurt

Split the bread lengthways and scoop out some of the centre to form a shell. Grate the bread to form rough crumbs, then mix them with the nuts and apple, and add the herbs and pepper to taste. Flake the mackerel and add it to the crumbs, then bind the mixture together with the yogurt, seasoning with salt.

Fill the bread shell with the mixture and chill before serving.

BAKED STUFFED
MACKEREL

Oatmeal and oily fish go together very well – it is a very traditional combination of ingredients. Use common thyme if you don't have lemon thyme, but reduce the quantity by half.

Serves 4

INGREDIENTS
4 mackerel, cleaned
Salt and freshly ground black
  pepper
1 small onion, finely chopped
60g/2oz butter
1 tbsp oatmeal
1 tbsp freshly chopped lemon
  thyme
1 tbsp freshly chopped parsley
60g/2oz fresh breadcrumbs
2-3 tbsps hot water

Preheat an oven to 190°C/375°F/ Gas Mark 5. Wash the mackerel, pat dry, then season lightly inside and out. Cook the onion in the butter until soft, then add all the remaining ingredients, binding the stuffing together with the water. Use to fill the mackerel, then wrap each fish in buttered foil and place in a roasting tin.

Bake the mackerel in the preheated oven for 30 minutes, then serve with green vegetables or a salad.

SAVOURY MACKEREL

In parts of Ireland the fishermen would boil their catch of mackerel in seawater. This recipe is prepared in a rather more conventional way.

Serves 4

INGREDIENTS
4 small to medium mackerel
30g/1oz seasoned flour
1 tbsp freshly chopped mixed
    herbs, or 1 tsp dried
Oil for shallow-frying
30g/1oz butter
1 tsp white wine vinegar
¼ tsp dry mustard
½ tsp anchovy essence
2 tbsps dry cider

Wash and clean the mackerel, then slice down the belly. Press the mackerel flat along their backbones, then turn them over and remove the bones.

Dip the prepared fish in the seasoned flour mixed with the herbs. Shallow-fry the fish, turning them carefully and allowing 5-6 minutes per side.

Melt the butter in a separate pan while the fish are cooking. Add the remaining ingredients, then bring the mixture slowly to the boil. Serve spooned over the hot mackerel.

PEPPERED MACKEREL WITH GOOSEBERRY SAUCE

Gooseberry sauce has been a popular accompaniment to mackerel since the 18th century – the tartness of the fruit cuts through any oiliness in the fish.

Serves 4

INGREDIENTS
4 mackerel fillets weighing about
   225g/8oz each
1 tbsp seasoned flour
Olive oil
2 tsps peppercorns, crushed

Marinade
3 tbsps oil
1 tbsp white wine vinegar
Grated rind and juice of 1 lemon
1 tbsp caster sugar

Gooseberry sauce
225g/8oz gooseberries, topped
   and tailed
1 dessert apple, peeled, cored and
   diced
60g/2oz sugar
Sprig of mint
150ml/¼ pint water
Pinch of salt
15g/½oz arrowroot (optional)

Mix the marinade ingredients together and pour over the mackerel in a shallow dish. Leave to marinate for 15-20 minutes.

Prepare the sauce by placing all the ingredients, except the arrowroot, in a pan and simmer together for 8-10 minutes, until the gooseberries are just beginning to burst. Remove the mint, then press the mixture through a sieve or blend in a liquidiser or food processor. Season to taste, then thicken the sauce, if desired, by adding the arrowroot made into a paste with a little water, and reboiling.

Dry the mackerel fillets on absorbent kitchen paper, then dip them in the seasoned flour and sprinkle with a little olive oil. Cook the mackerel fillets under a preheated grill for about 3 minutes on each side, then scatter the crushed peppercorns over them and serve with the gooseberry sauce.

SOUSED HERRINGS

Celtic peoples have valued the herring throughout history as a fish freely available to the poor. Nowadays, because of over-fishing, you almost have to be wealthy to afford a herring, but they are still very popular.

Serves 4

INGREDIENTS
4 large herrings
Salt and freshly ground black
    pepper
150ml/¼ pint water
150ml/¼ pint vinegar
1 blade mace
1 bayleaf
4 cloves
4 peppercorns

Preheat an oven to 180°C/350°F/
Gas Mark 4. Clean the herrings,
removing the heads, tails and fins.

Split the fish along the belly, then press flat and remove the backbones. Season the fish lightly, then roll up and secure with wooden cocktail sticks and place in a pie dish.

Heat the remaining ingredients together until almost boiling, then pour over the herrings, cover the dish and bake for 30-40 minutes, according to the size of the fish. Allow to cool, then chill the herrings in the cooking liquor until required.

BOILED LOBSTER

William Thackeray considered the perfect lobster to be three feet long! This recipe uses more affordable lobsters for a delicious starter.

Serves 4

INGREDIENTS
4 small lobsters, about 460g/1lb
  each
Salt or seaweed
250g/9oz butter, melted
Lemon wedges

Fill a large stock pot with water and add a good pinch of salt, or a piece of seaweed. Bring to the boil, then remove from the heat. Lower the live lobsters into the pot, keeping your hands well away from the claws – some fishermen or fishmongers will tie them for you. Lower them in claws first. Bring the water slowly back to the boil and cook for about 15 minutes, until they turn bright red.

Remove the cooked lobsters from the pan and drain briefly on absorbent kitchen paper. Crack the lobster shells along the underside and remove the stomach sac and lungs, but retain the liver or tomalley. Serve the lobster hot with plenty of melted butter for dipping, and lemon wedges for seasoning.

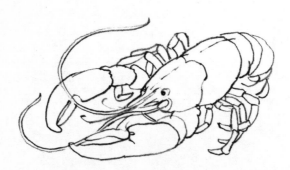

DRESSED CRAB

If you can buy your crab straight from the pot on the beach you will know it is as fresh as possible – it is always cheaper to buy a crab and dress it yourself. Chopped hard-boiled egg may be used with or in place of the chopped parsley to garnish the finished crab.

Serves 1-2

INGREDIENTS
1 large cooked crab
Lemon juice
Salt and freshly ground black
  pepper
Freshly chopped parsley

Prepare the crab. Break off the claws then turn the crab over and press up with the thumbs to separate the body from the shell. Cut the body into quarters and use a skewer to pick out the white meat. Discard the stomach sac and the lungs (dead man's fingers). Scrape out the brown meat from the shell. Crack the large claws and legs with a heavy weight and remove the meat. Shred the meat, discarding any shell or cartilage.

Scrub out the shell and dry it with absorbent kitchen paper. Season the white meat with a little lemon juice, salt and pepper. Place the brown meat in the centre of the shell, then divide the white meat between the spaces at either side. Garnish with chopped parsley between the meats.

MUSSELS IN WHITE WINE

Mussels have long been enjoyed in Ireland – it was said that mussels were the food of kings and limpets that of peasants. Cider may be substituted for wine in this recipe.

Serves 3-4

INGREDIENTS
1.8kg/4lbs live mussels
1 large onion, finely chopped
½ bottle dry white wine
15g/½oz butter
15g/½oz flour
Salt and freshly ground black
   pepper
Pinch of ground nutmeg
2 tbsps freshly chopped parsley

Wash and scrub the mussels well, pulling off any beards and discarding any whose shells are open and will not shut when lightly tapped. Place the mussels in a large pan with the onion and wine and bring to the boil. Cover and cook for 4-5 minutes, shaking frequently, until all the shells have opened – do not overcook the mussels or they will become tough.

Remove the mussels from the pan using a draining spoon and discard the top shells. Keep the mussels warm. Strain the cooking liquor into a clean pan and return it to the boil. Work the butter and flour together and gradually add the mixture to the pan, stirring constantly and boiling between each addition. Season to taste, then add the parsley and pour the sauce over the mussels. Serve with fresh soda bread.

SCALLOPS AU GRATIN

In the days when they were left to their own devices, scallops grew to a considerable size – it was said that they could reach up to four pounds in weight. Four scallops on a rather more conventional scale should suffice for this starter.

Serves 4

INGREDIENTS
4 large scallops
1 small onion, very finely chopped
2 tbsps olive oil
60g/2oz butter
120ml/4 fl oz white wine
2 egg yolks
2 tbsps double cream
60g/2oz Irish Cheddar, grated
4 tbsps fresh white breadcrumbs

Ask the fishmonger to leave the scallops on the deep half shells. Heat the oil and butter together in a large frying pan, add the onion and cook slowly until soft. Add the wine and bring to the boil. Remove the scallops from their shells, then slice the white parts and add them to the pan. Cook briskly for 1-2 minutes, then add the coral, sliced, and cook for a further 1 minute. Do not overcook or the scallops will toughen.

Rinse the scallop shells and dry them with kitchen paper. Remove the scallops from the pan with a slotted spoon and divide them between the shells. Cool the cooking liquor slightly, then stir in the egg yolks and heat gently to thicken the sauce, but do not boil. Add the cream, season the sauce to taste and pour it over the scallops. Mix the cheese and breadcrumbs together and scatter them over the sauce. Place the shells under a preheated grill and cook until just starting to brown. Serve piping hot with fresh brown bread.

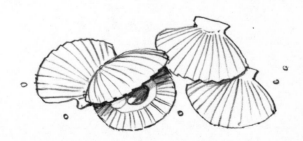

CURRIED PRAWN SALAD

Fresh prawns bought off the boat used to be one of the greatest treasure troves of a stroll along an Irish quayside. Though inferior in taste, frozen prawns are rather more convenient and affordable. Mixed with spices, they make for a deliciously piquant salad.

Serves 2-4

INGREDIENTS

225g/8oz frozen peeled prawns, defrosted
4 tbsps mayonnaise
2 tsps tomato purée
1 tsp curry paste
Salt and freshly ground black pepper
120-175g/4-6oz cooked rice
Lettuce for serving

Drain the prawns and shake them dry. Mix the mayonnaise with the tomato purée and curry paste, then season to taste. Combine the prawns, rice and dressing, then serve the salad arranged on shredded lettuce leaves. The salad may be garnished with egg, tomato and cucumber to make a more substantial main course for two.

SEAFOOD PANCAKES

The most popular filling for these pancakes is sole with a few scallops, but any fish may be used.

Serves 6

INGREDIENTS

680g/1½lbs mixed white fish, skinned
1 bay leaf
6 peppercorns
Salt
120g/4oz butter
1 onion, finely chopped
120g/4oz mushrooms, sliced
1 tbsp lemon juice
90g/3oz flour
120ml/4 fl oz white wine
Freshly grated nutmeg
150ml/¼ pint double or whipping cream, whipped
120g/4oz peeled prawns
12 thin pancakes

Place any fish trimmings in a pan with the bay leaf, peppercorns, a good pinch of salt and 570ml/1pint water. Bring to the boil then simmer for 20 minutes. Strain the stock into a clean pan.

Cut the white fish diagonally into 2.5cm/1-inch strips and poach in the stock for 2-3 minutes, removing the pieces with a slotted spoon. Strain the stock into a jug.

Melt 30g/1oz of the butter in a small pan and cook the onion until soft, then add the mushrooms and lemon juice and cook for 1-2 minutes, until the mushrooms have softened. Remove the onions and mushrooms from the pan and add the juices to the fish stock. Melt the remaining butter in the pan in which the fish was cooked, add the flour and cook for 1 minute without browning, then add the wine. Gradually add the fish and mushrooms stocks, stirring all the time, then return the pan to the heat and bring slowly to the boil. Cook for 1-2 minutes, until thickened, then remove from the heat and cool slightly before seasoning with salt, pepper and nutmeg and adding the cream.

Preheat an oven to 180°C/350°F/ Gas Mark 4. Use half the sauce to bind together the white fish, mushroom mixture and prawns, then use this to fill the pancakes, placing them in a buttered ovenproof dish. Pour the remaining sauce over the pancakes and bake for 30 minutes, until lightly browned.

IRISH FISH CAKES

With such a history of potato growing and the huge
variety of fish available from sea and river, it is inevitable
that the Irish have become famed for their fish cakes.
Good fish cakes use the same quantity of cooked flaked fish
to mashed potato – the better the fish, the less seasoning
will be required.

Serves 4

INGREDIENTS
680g/1½lbs cooked, flaked fish –
  use white fish, salmon or trout;
  oily fish is less successful in fish
  cakes
680g/1½lbs cooked mashed
  potato
30g/1oz butter
1-2 tbsps freshly chopped mixed
  herbs, including fennel and
  tarragon
Salt and freshly ground black
  pepper
3 eggs, size 3, beaten
Flour
120g/4oz fresh breadcrumbs
Oil for shallow-frying

Flake the fish, removing any skin
and bones, then mix it in a bowl
with the potato, butter and
seasonings. Bind the mixture
together with as much egg as
required, then, with floured
hands, shape it into four large or
eight medium fish cakes.

Dip the cakes in the remaining
egg, then coat them in the
breadcrumbs. Repeat the
procedure, using an extra egg if
necessary, then shallow-fry the
fish cakes in hot oil until golden
brown, turning once. Serve hot,
with tomato or caper sauce.

FISHERMAN'S PIE

Although delicious pies can be made using just one variety of fish, this is a traditional way of using up small amounts of many different kinds of fish. Most fish pie recipes include some shellfish, which gives extra flavour and texture. This recipe benefits from good fish – cheaper varieties will require more seasoning to give the finished pie some flavour.

Serves 4

INGREDIENTS
680g/1½lbs mixed white and
  smoked fish, skinned
45g/1½oz butter
45g/1½oz flour
430ml/¾ pint milk
Salt and freshly ground black
  pepper
2 tbsps freshly chopped parsley
120g/4oz peeled prawns
4 ripe tomatoes, sliced
460g/1lb cooked mashed potato
60g/2oz Irish Cheddar, grated

Preheat an oven to 200°C/400°F/
Gas Mark 6. Cut the fish into large
pieces and set aside. Melt the
butter in a pan, add the flour and
cook for 1 minute without
browning. Remove the pan from
the heat and gradually add the
milk. Return the pan to the heat
and bring the sauce gradually to
the boil, stirring all the time.
Simmer for 1 minute, then season
to taste and add the parsley.

Mix the prepared fish and prawns
carefully into the sauce, then turn
the mixture into a buttered
ovenproof dish. Arrange the
sliced tomatoes over the fish,
then top with the mashed potato
and scatter the cheese over it.
Bake for 30-40 minutes, until
browned.

MEAT

The Irish, like most Europeans, are great meat eaters, but this has not always been so. Traditionally, sheep and cattle were bred primarily for their wool and milk, and so it was the pig that supplemented the people's basic diet of grains and dairy products. Pork remains a popular meat to this day.

A Great Tradition of Pork Butchery

The pig is an animal that will forage for itself or can be fed on waste scraps of food. Being easy to keep, it is not surprising that it was the first animal to be domesticated in Ireland.

It has often been said that every single part of a pig can be used, leaving no wastage at all from the carcass. Salting and smoking have meant that joints could be cured to be used as hams and bacon at a later date. Pickled pork was also a popular dish, as was brawn. The pig was certainly an economical and reliable animal for country folk to keep, providing meat for everyday meals as well as for high days and holidays. For many years pork and bacon were the staple meats of both rich and poor. Not surprisingly, there are probably more traditional

114

recipes based on pork than on meat from any other animal.

Most villages and towns in Ireland would, until recently, have boasted a pork butcher specialising in fresh meat, as well as such delights as black pudding, sausages and hams. Regrettably, modern shopping trends and the advent of frozen, pre-packaged meat has meant that such emporiums now find it hard to survive, and a rich tradition of pork butchery is at risk of homogenisation from the standardised approach of the supermarket chains.

Lamb and Mutton – Ideal for the Pot
There is no breed of sheep that is truly native to Ireland, many having been cross-bred with varieties from Scotland or England to produce a hardier animal and a better carcass. Lamb and mutton have long been popular meats in Ireland – lamb for celebrations and mutton for everyday use. Irish lamb from coastal grazing has a flavour similar to the pré-salé lamb from the salt-marshes of the Cherbourg peninsula. The meat is characterized by a marvellous flavour, with the salt balancing any fattiness in the meat. Such lamb should be savoured, and benefits from simple preparation – roasting is the perfect method of cooking.

Lamb is a very versatile meat. In the days before domestic ovens it had the advantage of being relatively quick to cook and of open texture, and therefore well suited to being braised, boiled or pot-roasted over an open fire. Although mutton takes longer to cook, it benefits from long, slow cooking and was therefore a good meat for the pot. Today, mutton is in relatively short supply, although it should not be disregarded as part of the modern diet – excess fat can be trimmed before cooking and the flavour of mutton is often better than that of lamb. Many traditional mutton dishes have now been adapted for use with lamb to meet modern demands for leaner meat and dishes that are quick to cook.

Irish Stew – a Much Maligned Speciality
Lamb or mutton chops have always been used for one of the most traditional, yet most maligned, of Irish dishes – Irish Stew. Cooked with care using quality ingredients it can provide a veritable feast. The secret of a successful stew is to avoid a watery consistency – the potatoes should be cooked with the lamb to absorb much of the liquid. With the current interest in tasty

varieties of potato, it should be possible for everyone to produce an Irish stew that is truly special.

Spiced Beef to Celebrate

Beef has only recently enjoyed widespread popularity in Ireland. For many years the prime purpose of cattle was to produce milk for cheese and butter making. A cow, or more usually an unwanted bull calf, was occasionally slaughtered and butchered to produce meat for the table. It was important to deal with the meat before the weather became hot, and many cuts were actually salted for later use or for giving away to estate workers. Corned or preserved beef was a popular dish with the poor. Today beef plays an important part in festive menus across Ireland and one of the most famous dishes is the spiced beef that is sold at Christmas. It is easy to prepare at home, but the most essential ingredient is one that is no longer common – time. Spiced beef is very similar to pastrami – a popular American delicatessen meat – the main difference being that a pastrami is smoked at the end of its spicing.

The meat industry is now a major source of export income for Ireland, but the Irish themselves remain great meat eaters and many people, both young and old, still consider a meal to be incomplete if it doesn't include a meat dish.

IRISH STEW

*This is one of the most famous and yet most maligned of
traditional Irish dishes. If your previous experience of this
classic has been disappointing, please try this recipe.*

Serves 4

INGREDIENTS
900g/2lbs boned mutton or lamb,
  or
  1.4kg/3lbs best end cutlets
900g/2lbs potatoes, peeled and
  sliced
2 large onions, sliced
1 tbsp freshly chopped thyme
1 tbsp freshly chopped parsley
Salt and freshly ground black
  pepper
430ml/¾ pint water

Trim the meat, leaving just a little
of the fat on the bones. Layer the
meat, potatoes and onions in a
large saucepan, starting and
finishing with a layer of potatoes
and seasoning each layer with the
herbs, salt and pepper. Pour the
water into the pan and cover with
a tight-fitting lid.

Simmer the stew very slowly for 2-
2½ hours, shaking the pan
occasionally to prevent the
potatoes from sticking. Add extra
water, if necessary, to prevent the
stew from drying out. The
finished stew should not be
watery as the potatoes will help
thicken it.

STUFFED BREAST OF LAMB

It is not difficult to remove the bones from a breast of lamb, but if you do not have a strong meat knife you will find it easier to ask the butcher to do it for you. A home-made stuffing turns this simple dish into a real treat.

Serves 4

INGREDIENTS
120g/4oz fresh white
　breadcrumbs
60g/2oz suet, chopped or
　shredded
1 onion, finely chopped
1 tsp freshly chopped marjoram
1 tsp freshly chopped thyme
Grated rind of ½ a lemon
Salt and freshly ground black
　pepper
1 egg, size 3, beaten
1 breast of lamb, boned
1 tbsp flour

Preheat an oven to 200°C/400°F/
Gas Mark 6. Mix the breadcrumbs, suet, onion, herbs and lemon rind with a little salt and pepper, and bind with the beaten egg. Spread the stuffing mixture over the lamb, then roll up, starting at the wider end, and tie securely with string.

Place the lamb in a small roasting tin and roast for 1 hour. Remove the meat from the tin and keep warm while making the gravy. Drain off any excess fat, then stir the flour into the meat juices in the tin. Add about 280ml/½ pint stock or vegetable water and bring slowly to the boil, stirring constantly. Season to taste, then serve the gravy poured over the sliced lamb.

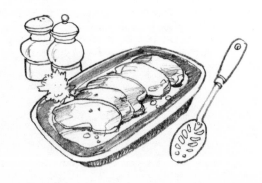

ROAST HERBED
LEG OF LAMB

Leg is the easiest of roasting cuts to carve. The herb and breadcrumb coating absorbs any fattiness from the meat.

Serves 6

INGREDIENTS
1.6kg/3½lb leg of lamb
2 bay leaves
120g/4oz butter
225g/8oz fresh breadcrumbs
1 tbsp freshly chopped mixed herbs
Juice of 2 lemons
Salt and freshly ground black pepper

Preheat an oven to 200°C/400°F/ Gas Mark 6 and prepare a sheet of foil large enough to wrap around the meat completely.

Place the lamb in the centre of the foil on top of the bay leaves. Mix the butter with the remaining ingredients and spread over the lamb using a wet palette knife. Loosely wrap the foil around the meat and transfer it to a roasting tin. Roast for 1-1½ hours, depending on how pink you like your lamb.

Half an hour before the end of cooking time, unwrap the foil and baste the meat with the butter in the bottom of the parcel. Return the lamb to the oven, uncovered, and cook for the remaining time, until the crust is brown and crisp. Allow the lamb to stand for 10 minutes before carving.

119

GUARD OF HONOUR WITH APRICOT STUFFING

This is one of the most spectacular ways to serve roast lamb. The best ends must, however, be the same size for the "guard of honour" to be balanced.

Serves 6

INGREDIENTS
2 best ends of neck, each
    weighing about 900g/2lbs,
    French trimmed and chined
Seasoned flour

Apricot stuffing
30g/1oz butter
1 small onion, finely chopped
175g/6oz ready-to-eat dried
    apricots, chopped
120g/4oz fresh white
    breadcrumbs
60g/2oz blanched almonds,
    chopped
2 tbsps freshly chopped parsley
Salt and freshly ground black
    pepper
Juice of ½ a lemon
1-2 eggs, lightly beaten

Preheat an oven to 200°C/400°F/
Gas Mark 6. Melt the butter for
the stuffing, add the onions and
cook slowly until soft. Remove the
pan from the heat and stir in the
chopped apricots, breadcrumbs,
almonds, seasonings and lemon
juice, then add sufficient beaten
egg to bind the mixture together.

Stand the racks of lamb up facing
each other, with the skin sides
outwards and interlock the bones.
Fill the centre with the stuffing
mixture. Tie the racks loosely
together in two or three places,
tying between the bones to keep
the joint together. Wrap small
pieces of foil around the exposed
bones, then place the joint in a
roasting tin. Dust the meat with a
little seasoned flour – this will
help to crisp the fat during
cooking.

Roast in the preheated oven for
15 minutes, then reduce the heat
to 180°C/350°F/Gas Mark 4 and
cook for a further 40-60 minutes,
depending on how rare you like
your lamb. Remove to a warmed
serving dish and allow to stand for
10 minutes before removing the
string and carving. The meat
juices may be made into a gravy
by mixing with flour and a little
vegetable water.

LAMB RAGOUT

*This rich stew sounds extravagant, but it is quite economical
when made with breast of lamb.*

Serves 4

INGREDIENTS
900g/2lbs boneless breast of lamb
1 clove garlic, crushed
15g/½oz butter
280ml/½ pint stock
½ tsp salt
1 tsp freshly chopped marjoram
12 button onions
460g/1lb tomatoes, quartered
Freshly ground black pepper

Cut the meat into 5cm/2-inch pieces and trim off any fat. Brown the meat in the butter with the garlic in a large pan, then add the stock, which should barely cover the meat. Season the ragout with the salt and marjoram, then cover and simmer slowly for 45 minutes, until almost tender.

Stir the onions into the pan and cook for a further 45 minutes before adding the tomatoes. Cook for just 10 minutes, until the tomatoes are soft, then season to taste and serve with baked potatoes.

BOILED MUTTON

Mutton appeared regularly on the menus of most Irish households in days gone by. It is less common now, as the modern preference for leaner meat dictates that lambs are slaughtered when young and lean. However, mutton does have a delicious flavour and makes a welcome change when served with caper sauce (see page 85).

Weigh the mutton and allow 20 minutes per 460g/1lb plus 20 minutes over. Plunge the joint into a pan containing enough boiling, salted water to cover the joint, return it to the boil and boil rapidly for 5 minutes. Reduce the heat and simmer for the remaining cooking time. Remove the joint from the water and allow it to stand for 5-10 minutes before carving and serving with the caper sauce.

HARICOT MUTTON

This is a simple traditional stew made from classic ingredients. Although time consuming, it makes for an ideal family meal. Use lamb if you prefer.

Serves 4

INGREDIENTS
120g/4oz haricot beans, soaked
  overnight
900g/2lbs boneless breast or neck
  fillet of mutton
30g/1oz dripping or butter
Salt and freshly ground black
  pepper
2 carrots, chopped
2 white turnips, chopped
2 onions, sliced
Stock or water
Freshly chopped parsley

Preheat an oven to 160°C/325°F/ Gas Mark 3. Drain the beans and rinse them in fresh water. Cut the meat into small pieces and brown well on all sides in the dripping, then place in a casserole dish and season.

Add the prepared vegetables to the fat in the pan and cook until soft and slightly browned, then add them to the meat with the beans. Add sufficient stock to barely cover the meat, then cover the casserole and cook for about 2½ hours, until the meat is tender. Season to taste and garnish with chopped parsley before serving.

SAVOURY CHOPS

*Even today lamb chops are quite a luxurious cut. This
savoury topping makes a welcome change from serving
them with mint sauce.*

Serves 2-4

INGREDIENTS
4 loin chops of lamb
1 clove garlic
30g/1oz butter
1 tbsp freshly chopped mixed
    herbs, parsley, thyme and
    tarragon
Salt and freshly ground black
    pepper
2 tbsps fresh breadcrumbs

Trim the chops and rub them with
the cut surface of the clove of
garlic. Melt the butter, then mix it
with the herbs and some
seasoning. Dip the chops into the
butter and then into the
breadcrumbs.

Preheat a grill, then grill the chops
for about 5 minutes on each side.

LIVER WITH ONIONS

*In Medieval times plenty of herbs were added to this dish to
disguise the rather strong flavour of the liver. This recipe uses
lamb's liver, which has a relatively mild flavour.*

Serves 4-6

INGREDIENTS
460g/1lb lamb's liver, trimmed and
    thinly sliced
45g/1½oz seasoned flour
60g/2oz butter
460g/1lb onions, thinly sliced
2 tbsps freshly chopped parsley

Dip the liver in the seasoned
flour, coating it evenly. Melt the
butter in a large frying-pan, add
the onion and fry until lightly
browned. Add the liver to the pan
and cook for 2-3 minutes on each
side – the exact cooking time will
depend on the thickness of the
liver slices. Add the parsley and
serve the liver and onions
immediately.

LIVER & BACON WITH TOMATOES & RED WINE SAUCE

This is a contemporary Irish dish – liver and bacon brought up to date!

Serves 4

INGREDIENTS
1 large onion, chopped
3 tbsps olive oil
8 thin slices lamb's liver
30g/1oz seasoned flour
150ml/¼ pint red wine
400g/14oz can chopped tomatoes
6 basil leaves, torn into small
  pieces
1 tsp clear honey
Salt and freshly ground black
  pepper
4 rashers streaky bacon, rinded
225g/8oz pasta shells or macaroni

Preheat an oven to 190°C/375°F/ Gas Mark 5. Cook the onion in the oil until soft, then remove it to a large, flat ovenproof casserol edish with a slotted spoon.

Dredge the liver with the seasoned flour, brown it lightly in the oil in the pan, then lay the liver on top of the onions. Stir any remaining flour into the pan juices, add the red wine, all but 2 tbsps of the tomatoes, the basil and the honey. Bring to the boil, season to taste, then pour the sauce over the liver. Cut the bacon rashers in half lengthways, then lay them on top of the casserole. Bake, uncovered, in the hot oven for 20-25 minutes.

Boil the pasta in plenty of salted water for 15 minutes, or as directed on the packet. Drain well, add the remaining tomatoes and season lightly. Serve the liver on a bed of pasta.

KIDNEYS WITH BACON

*Kidneys were once regarded as a food of the poor, but by
Victorian times and in the age of lavish Irish country
house entertaining, they were very much the breakfast
food of the rich.*

Serves 4

INGREDIENTS

460g/1lb lamb's kidneys
3 tbsps sherry
2 tbsps oil
8 lean rashers bacon, rinded and
  chopped
1 onion, chopped
1 tbsp tomato chutney
1 tbsp Worcestershire sauce
2 tbsps water
Salt and freshly ground black
  pepper
1 tbsp cornflour
2 tbsps freshly chopped parsley

Cut the kidneys in half and remove
the cores, then cut a lattice
pattern into the back of each
piece, taking care not to cut right
through. Marinate the kidneys in
the sherry for 15 minutes.

Heat the oil in a large frying-pan
and cook the bacon and onion
slowly for 5 minutes, then remove
from the pan with a slotted
spoon. Add the kidneys to the
pan, reserving the sherry
marinade, and cook quickly for 3
minutes. Stir the chutney,
Worcestershire sauce and water
into the pan, then add the bacon
and onions, season lightly and
cook slowly for 5 minutes.

Blend the cornflour with the
sherry marinade, then stir the
mixture into the kidneys and
continue stirring until boiling and
thickened. Garnish with the
chopped parsley and serve at
once.

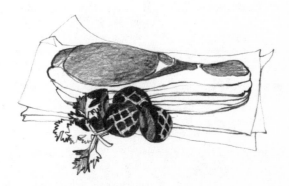

BEEF STEW & DUMPLINGS

The residents of Tipperary call this Irish stew, although the traditional Irish stew is made with lamb and potatoes! Dumplings have long been used in Irish cookery, both in soups and stews.

Serves 4-6

INGREDIENTS
460-680g/1-1½lbs stewing steak
30g/1oz dripping or butter
2 onions, chopped
4 carrots, sliced
1 bay leaf
30g/1oz seasoned flour
850ml/1½ pints beef stock
1 tbsp freshly chopped herbs
Salt and freshly ground black
    pepper

Dumplings
175g/6oz self-raising flour
½ tsp salt
90g/3oz shredded suet
Water to mix

Preheat an oven to 160°C/325°F/ Gas Mark 3. Cut the beef into cubes, removing any excess fat. Heat half the butter in a flameproof casserole dish, add the onions, carrots and bay leaf and cook until softened, then remove them with a slotted spoon. Toss the beef in the seasoned flour, add the remaining butter to the pan, then fry the meat in batches to brown it on all sides.

Return the vegetables to the pan, gradually add the stock, then season with the herbs, salt and pepper. Bring to the boil, then cover with a tight-fitting lid and cook in the oven for 2½ hours, until the meat is tender.

Make the dumplings towards the end of the cooking time. Sift the flour and salt into a basin, stir in the suet and mix into a soft dough with cold water. Divide into 8 and roll into dumplings with floured hands. Add to the simmering stew 20 minutes before the end of the cooking period. Serve the stew as soon as the dumplings are cooked.

SPICED BEEF

At Christmas time Irish butchers' windows are full of spiced beef, often tied with ribbons and decorated with holly. It is easy to prepare at home, but does require quite a lot of time and care.

Serves 20

INGREDIENTS
1 large clove garlic
460g/1lb cooking salt
3 bay leaves, finely chopped
1 tsp powdered mace
½ tsp ground cloves
1 tsp crushed black peppercorns
1 tsp allspice
2 tbsps black treacle
45g/1½oz brown sugar
2.7kg/6lb piece of brisket,
   silverside or topside

Crush the garlic into a paste with a little of the salt, then mix the paste with all the other ingredients. Place the beef in a large dish and rub the spices all over it. Repeat this process every day for a week, gathering the spices up from the bottom of the dish with any juices that have collected there. Keep the beef in a cool larder or refrigerator during this time.

Tie the meat up firmly and rub with an extra 1 tsp of ground cloves if wished. Place in a pan, cover with cold water and simmer slowly for 6 hours. Allow the beef to cool for an hour or so in the cooking liquid, then remove it to a suitable dish, cover with a plate and press under a heavy weight. Chill thoroughly and slice very thinly before serving.

BEEF IN GUINNESS

*Traditional Irish stout makes a wonderful cooking liquor
for beef, and this casserole is truly rich in flavour.
If you use braising steak or topside, reduce the cooking
time by about a third.*

Serves 4

INGREDIENTS
680g/1½lbs shin of beef
2 onions, sliced
225g/8oz carrots, sliced
3 tbsps olive oil
45g/1½oz seasoned flour
150ml/¼ pint Guinness
150ml/¼ pint stock or water
6 basil leaves, torn into pieces
Salt and freshly ground black
   pepper
1 tsp clear honey

Preheat an oven to 160°C/325°F/
Gas Mark 3. Cut the beef into
large dice, about 12 pieces. Cook
the onions and carrots in the oil
until soft, then transfer them to a
casserole dish with a slotted spoon.

Toss the beef in the seasoned
flour, then brown it on all sides in
the remaining oil over a high heat
and add it to the onions and
carrots in the casserole dish.
Brown the beef in two lots if
necessary.

Heat the Guinness and stock
together in the pan, then add the
basil, seasonings and honey. Pour
over the beef, then cover the
casserole with a tight fitting lid
and cook in the preheated oven
for 1½ hours. Season to taste
before serving.

This casserole benefits from being
reheated the following day –
standing overnight allows the
flavours to develop.

BEEF OLIVES

These rolls of beef around a savoury stuffing first appeared on banquet menus in the Middle Ages and have been popular ever since. Beef olives are often sold ready-prepared, but it is much more satisfying to make them yourself, using you own stuffing.

Serves 4

INGREDIENTS

8 thin beef steaks for frying, each about 10x15cm/4x6 inches
30g/1oz shredded suet
2 rashers streaky bacon, rinded and chopped
120g/4oz fresh white breadcrumbs
1 tbsp freshly chopped parsley
Grated rind of ½ lemon
Salt and freshly ground black pepper
1 egg, size 3, beaten
2 tbsps seasoned flour
30g/1oz butter
430ml/¾ pint beef stock
2 tbsps sherry

Preheat an oven to 180°C/350°F/ Gas Mark 4. Place the steaks between two sheets of silicone paper and pound them flat. Mix the suet, bacon, breadcrumbs, parsley, mixed herbs, lemon rind and seasonings together, then bind with the beaten egg.

Divide the stuffing between the eight pieces of beef, then roll up and secure each olive with string. Dust each one with the seasoned flour, then fry in the butter until browned on all sides. Transfer the olives to a casserole dish, then stir the stock into the residue left in the pan, bring gradually to the boil, add the sherry and pour the sauce over the olives in the dish. Cover and cook in the oven for 45-50 minutes.

Carefully transfer the beef olives to a warmed serving plate, cutting away the strings. Reduce the sauce to a coating consistency by rapid boiling, if necessary, then pour it over the beef and serve.

ROAST RIBS OF BEEF

Lamb may be the traditional meat of Ireland, but roast beef is very popular and this is one of the best ways of serving it.

Serves 6-8

INGREDIENTS
2.3 kg/5lb forerib of beef on the bone
Lard or butter
Salt and freshly ground black pepper
1 tbsp flour
280ml/½ pint beef stock

Preheat an oven to 220°C/425°F/ Gas Mark 7. Place the beef on a rack in a large roasting tin and rub the meat with a little softened lard or butter. Season with black pepper, then roast in the preheated oven for 15-20 minutes, to sear the meat.

Reduce the oven temperature to 200°C/400°F/Gas Mark 6 and cook the beef for a further 1¼-1½ hours, depending on how well done you like your beef. Baste regularly with the meat juices.

Remove the beef and allow it to stand for 10 minutes before carving. Pour any excess fat from the tin, stir the flour into the meat juices and cook until browned, then add the stock. Bring the gravy slowly to the boil, stirring continuously, then season to taste and simmer for 2-3 minutes. Serve the gravy with the sliced beef.

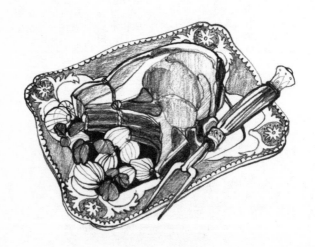

POT ROAST BEEF

This has long been a popular method of roasting the cheaper cuts of meat – it works well with chuck or 'round' steak, as the Irish call it, but remember to ask the butcher to leave the meat in one piece.

Serves 6

INGREDIENTS

1.4kg/3lb piece chuck or 'round' steak
1 clove garlic
2 tbsps seasoned flour
45g/1½oz beef dripping or butter
1 onion, chopped
570ml/1 pint beef stock
1 tbsp freshly chopped herbs
Salt and freshly ground black pepper

Rub the meat all over with the cut edge of a clove of garlic, then toss the joint in the seasoned flour. Heat the fat in a heavy-based saucepan and cook the onions until lightly browned, then remove them from the pan with a slotted spoon. Add the meat and brown it quickly on all sides. Add stock to a depth of 1.25cm/½ inch, then cover the pan with a tight-fitting lid.

Simmer the meat slowly, until tender – this will take about 3 hours. Add extra stock from time to time so that the pan does not boil dry. The onions should be returned to the pan 30 minutes before the meat is done.

Serve the beef sliced with creamy mashed potato.

131

STEAK & KIDNEY PIE

This has been a favourite dish since the Middle Ages, when in Ireland it would certainly have had oysters added to it. You may prefer to use canned oysters now, or sliced mushrooms.

Serves 4-6

INGREDIENTS

680g/1½lbs rump or braising
   steak
175g/6oz kidney
60g/2oz butter
2 medium onions, finely chopped
30g/1oz seasoned flour
430-570ml/¾-1 pint beef stock
120g/4oz oysters or mushrooms
   (canned oysters work well)
400g/14oz prepared puff pastry
Salt and freshly ground black
   pepper
Beaten egg for glazing

Preheat an oven to 150°C/300°F/ Gas Mark 2. Trim the steak and cut into bite-sized pieces, then core and chop the kidney. Heat half the butter in a flameproof casserole dish, add the onions and cook until soft, then remove with a slotted spoon. Toss the steak in half the seasoned flour, then brown it all over in the butter, adding butter as necessary. Remove the steak from the pan, toss the kidneys in the remaining flour, then brown in the same way.

Return the steak and onions to the pan, adding any remaining flour, then gradually add the stock. Bring to the boil, then cover and cook in the oven for 1½ hours, or until the meat is tender. Allow the meat to cool.

Preheat an oven to 220°C/425°F/ Gas Mark 7. Add the oysters or mushrooms to the cold meat, then transfer to a suitable pie dish together with 150ml/¼ pint of the gravy. Place a pastry funnel in the centre of the dish.

Roll the pastry out to cover the dish, then trim strips of pastry to line the lip of the pie dish. Dampen them with water, cover the dish with the pastry lid, then seal the pastry edges together and flute them with your fingers. Glaze the pastry with the beaten egg, then bake the pie for 15 minutes. Lower the oven temperature to 180°C/350°F/Gas Mark 4 and continue cooking for a further 30-40 minutes. Reheat the remaining gravy and serve it separately.

BRAISED OXTAIL

Oxen were once used extensively for pulling ploughs and carts as they are much stronger than horses. Oxtail went out of fashion for a while, but it has recently become very popular again – it requires a long, slow cook and is better reheated the next day. The flavour is superb.

Serves 4

INGREDIENTS
900g-1.15kg/2-2½lbs oxtail, jointed
2 tbsps seasoned flour
30g/1oz dripping or lard
2 large onions, finely sliced
2 carrots, sliced
1 rasher bacon, rinded and diced
Salt and freshly ground black pepper
2 bay leaves
2 stalks parsley
4 cloves
430ml/¾ pint beef or game stock
150ml/¼ pint red wine

Preheat an oven to 160°C/325°F/ Gas Mark 3. Dredge the oxtail pieces with the seasoned flour, then fry them in the fat until browned all over. Remove the oxtail with a slotted spoon, then brown the prepared vegetables and bacon in the oil.

Place half the vegetables in an ovenproof casserole dish, lay the oxtail on top and cover with the remaining vegetables. Add the seasonings, stock and wine to the pan, bring to the boil, then pour the mixture over the meat and vegetables. Cover the casserole and cook slowly for 2½-3 hours, until the oxtail is tender.

If you allow the meat to stand overnight you will be able to skim the fat from the top of the casserole before reheating.

STEAK & KIDNEY PUDDING

Like steak and kidney pie, this pudding would traditionally have included oysters – canned oysters may be used if fresh oysters are too expensive. I can think of nothing more welcoming on a cold winter's day than a piping hot steak and kidney pudding.

Serves 4-6

Ingredients

Pastry
340g/12oz self-raising flour
Pinch of salt
175g/6oz shredded suet
Cold water to mix

Filling
680g/1½lbs stewing steak, diced
225g/8oz kidney, cored and diced
2 tbsps seasoned flour
175g/6oz mushrooms, sliced or
  250g/10oz can oysters, drained
280ml/½ pint beef stock

Sieve together the flour and salt for the pastry, then stir in the suet and bind together with cold water. Knead lightly, then roll out into a large circle on a floured surface. Cut away one quarter of the pastry and keep it to make the lid of the pudding. Use the remaining pastry to line a 1.4-1.7-litre/2½-3 pint pudding basin.

Toss the prepared steak and kidney in the seasoned flour, then place half the mixture in the lined pudding basin. Cover with the mushrooms or oysters in a layer and top with the remaining meat. Pour sufficient stock into the basin so that it comes to within 2.5cm/1 inch of the top of the meat, roll out the remaining pastry to make a lid for the pudding, damp the edges and seal the layers of pastry together.

Cover the pudding with greased greaseproof paper and foil, and tie it securely in place with string. Stand the basin on a trivet in a large pan of water, cover the pan and steam gently for 4 hours. Add extra water from time to time and do not allow the pan to boil dry.

Serve the pudding with a whiskey-flavoured, grainy mustard.

HUNTSMAN'S SANDWICH

*A sizzling steak sandwich served with flavoured
Irish mustard.*

Serves 2

INGREDIENTS
15g/½oz butter
1 onion, sliced
2 tbsps oil
2 thin fillet steaks
Irish whiskey mustard
Salt and freshly ground black
    pepper
2 round, crusty rolls

Cook the onion in the butter until browned, then remove it with a slotted spoon. Add the oil to the pan and leave until hot; add the steaks and cook quickly on both sides – allow 3-4 minutes total cooking time, according to how you like your steak.

Spread the rolls with mustard, divide the onions between them, then top with the steaks. Season lightly and serve either piping hot or cold.

PORK CISTE

*This is a very traditional dish, although sadly out of fashion.
Ciste means cake and refers to a suet-crust topping.*

Serves 6

INGREDIENTS
60g/2oz butter
1 tbsp oil
2 pork kidneys, cored and
  chopped
1 large onion, chopped
3 carrots, sliced
6 pork chops
1 cooking apple, peeled, cored
  and sliced
1 tbsp freshly chopped parsley
1 tsp freshly chopped thyme
Salt and freshly ground black
  pepper
570ml/1 pint dry cider

Ciste
225g/8oz self-raising flour
Pinch of salt
120g/4oz shredded suet
90g/3oz sultanas
Water to mix

Heat the butter and oil together in a large flameproof casserole dish, add the kidneys and brown on all sides, then remove with a slotted spoon. Add the prepared vegetables to the casserole and cook until lightly browned, then add them to the kidneys. Brown the chops lightly on both sides and arrange them in the casserole, then cover with the kidney and vegetable mixture, the cooking apple and herbs. Season well and add sufficient cider to cover the vegetables. Cover the casserole with a tight-fitting lid and simmer slowly for 30 minutes.

Prepare the suet crust by mixing the flour, salt, suet and sultanas together, then add sufficient cold water to form a soft dough. Knead on a lightly floured surface, then roll out to fit the top of the casserole. Lay the crust on top of the meat, then cover again and simmer for a further 1½ hours.

Serve by cutting the crust into 6 and spooning the meat and vegetables out to accompany it. This dish may also be baked in a moderate oven at 180°C/350°F/ Gas Mark 4.

PORK PIE

Pork pies were traditionally served to huntsmen at the end of a hard day's riding.

Serves 4-6

INGREDIENTS

Stock
570ml/1 pint water
Pork or veal bones, or 1 pig's
   trotter
1 bay leaf
1 onion
Salt
4 peppercorns

Filling
120g/4oz streaky bacon, rinded
   and chopped
680g/1½lbs pork fillet, diced
Salt and freshly ground black
   pepper
Pinch of dry mustard
3 fresh sage leaves, finely
   chopped
1 tbsp hot water

Pastry
340g/12oz plain flour
½ tsp salt
150g/5oz lard
150ml/¼ pint water and milk,
   mixed
1 egg, beaten, for glazing

Simmer all the stock ingredients together for 3 hours, then strain and return the liquid to the pan. Boil rapidly until reduced to 280ml/½ pint, then leave to cool. Mix all the ingredients for the filling together and put to one side.

Preheat an oven to 180°C/350°F/ Gas Mark 4. Sieve the flour and salt for the pastry into a bowl. Heat the lard and water together until the lard has melted, then bring to a rapid boil and pour into the flour. Mix rapidly with a wooden spoon, then turn out onto a floured surface and knead until smooth. Cover with an upturned bowl and leave to cool slightly. Mould two-thirds of the pastry into a 17.5 cm/7-inch spring-form tin. Pack the filling mixture into the pastry case, then roll out the remaining pastry to form a lid. Damp the edges with water then cover the pie, sealing the pastry together. Make a slit in the middle of the lid with a sharp knife and decorate with pastry leaves made out of any trimmings. Glaze the pie with beaten egg then bake for 1½-2 hours – remove the sides of the tin after one hour and glaze the pie frequently from that time onwards.

Allow the pie to cool. Warm the jellied stock then pour it into the pie through a small funnel. Chill the pie in the fridge before slicing to serve.

CRUBEENS

This is the original Irish take-away! Crubeens are simply pig's trotters, boiled for hours – they are very popular in traditional Irish pubs.

Serves 4

INGREDIENTS
4 pig's trotters
1 onion, chopped
1 carrot, sliced
Salt
6 peppercorns
1 bay leaf
Sprig of thyme
Sprig of parsley

Place the trotters in a pan with the vegetables and seasonings. Add sufficient cold water to cover the trotters, then bring slowly to the boil and simmer for 3 hours.

Crubeens are finger food – the meat should be sucked from the bones. When cold, they become coated with a thick jelly. It is said that there is more meat on a hind trotter.

DUBLIN CODDLE

This is a Saturday night special in Dublin pubs, where it is generally washed down with a pint or two of Guinness.

Serves 4

INGREDIENTS
460g/1lb thick pork sausages
4 rashers thickly sliced bacon, rinded
460g/1lb onions, sliced
680g/1½lbs potatoes, sliced
Salt and freshly ground black pepper to taste

Place the sausages and bacon in a frying pan with enough water to cover; bring to the boil and simmer for 5 minutes. Drain and reserve the cooking liquid, then add the sliced onions and potatoes to the pan with plenty of seasoning. Cover with the reserved liquid, lay a piece of greaseproof paper over the potatoes and cover the pan with a tight-fitting lid. Simmer the coddle slowly for about 1 hour, shaking the pan from time to time to prevent the contents from sticking.

ROAST LOIN OF PORK WITH SAGE & ONION STUFFING BALLS

The pig was the first animal to be domesticated in Ireland so pork has been a traditional meat for centuries. Pigs would have been spit roasted whole for special occasions, but a roast such as this would only have been possible since the domestic oven became commonplace.

Serves 6

INGREDIENTS
1.4kg/3lb loin of pork, scored
  deeply
Salt

Stuffing
45g/1½oz butter
225g/8oz onions, finely chopped
Stock or water
1 tbsp freshly chopped sage
120g/4oz fresh breadcrumbs
Salt and freshly ground black
  pepper
1 egg, size 3, beaten

Preheat an oven to 190°C/375°F/ Gas Mark 5. Place the pork in a roasting tin with the crackling uppermost, and sprinkle the surface with salt. Roast the pork for 1¾-2 hours, turning the oven up to 200°C/400°F/Gas Mark 6 for the last 15 minutes to crisp the crackling.

While the meat is cooking, melt the butter in a small saucepan, add the onions and cook until lightly browned. Add just enough water or stock to cover the onions, then simmer for 15 minutes. Remove the pan from the heat and add the sage, breadcrumbs and seasonings. Cool slightly, then bind the stuffing together with the beaten egg.

Shape the stuffing into balls, then cook them around the meat for the last 30 minutes of cooking time.

PORK & PEASE PUDDING

It is now more common to serve pease pudding with gammon, but it was traditionally served with pickled pork.

Serves 8

INGREDIENTS

225g/8oz yellow split peas, soaked overnight
1.8kg/4lb pickled hand and spring of pork
1 onion, sliced
2 carrots, sliced
2 small turnips, diced
4 sticks celery, chopped
Sprig of sage
Sprig of parsley
Sprig of thyme
30g/1oz butter
1 egg yolk
Salt and freshly ground black pepper

Place the pork in a large saucepan with the vegetables. Tie the soaked split peas loosely in a large piece of muslin, allowing plenty of room for them to swell. Hang the bundle in the pan with the pork and tie it to the handle with string. Add the herbs and enough water to cover the meat; bring to the boil and skim off any scum. Reduce the heat, cover and simmer for about 2 hours, until the pork is tender.

Remove the cooked pork from the pan and keep it warm. Remove the muslin bag and squeeze it thoroughly to drain and dry the peas, then pass them through a sieve or purée them in a liquidiser or food processor. Turn the purée into a clean pan over a gentle heat, then beat in the butter and egg yolk. Season to taste, but do not allow the pudding to boil.

Strain some of the broth from the pork to use as gravy, then slice the meat and arrange it on a serving dish. Serve the pease pudding separately. The vegetables may be served with the meat or made into a soup with the remaining stock.

LIMERICK HAM

Limerick ham has been famous throughout the world since the 18th century because of its fine juniper flavouring, imparted during the smoking process. Use smoked gammon for this recipe if Limerick ham is not available.

Serves 10

INGREDIENTS

1 smoked gammon, weighing about 2.3-2.7kg/5-6lbs
1 onion
10 cloves
6 peppercorns
1 tbsp clear honey

Soak the gammon for at least 12 hours, then rinse it and place in a pan of fresh water with the onion, stuck with the cloves. Add the peppercorns and honey, bring the water to the boil, then simmer the ham, allowing 20 minutes per 460g/1lb plus 20 minutes over. The ham is cooked when the thick skin peels off easily.

Peel away the skin and allow the ham to cool before serving. Serve sliced. The ham may be coated with breadcrumbs or glazed with equal quantities of sieved apricot jam, brown sugar and vinegar and roasted for 30-40 minutes at 180°C/350°F/Gas Mark 4 after simmering.

BAKED HAM WITH APPLES

Most people serve ham or gammon steaks with pineapple,
but the traditional Irish accompaniment is apple – use
Bramleys, or a dessert apple such as a Granny Smith.

Serves 2

INGREDIENTS
2 slices of cooked smoked ham,
   about 2.5cm/1 inch thick
6 cloves
4 tbsps brown sugar
2 tbsps Irish mustard with
   whiskey
1-2 tbsps oil
1 large cooking apple, peeled,
   cored and sliced
¼ tsp ground cinnamon
¼ tsp ground cloves
150ml/¼ pint cider or apple juice

Preheat an oven to 180°C/350°F/
Gas Mark 4. Stick the fatty side of
the ham with cloves, then mix
together the sugar and mustard
and smear the mixture over the
ham. Heat the oil in a frying-pan
and sear the ham on both sides
until well browned, then transfer
it to an ovenproof casserole dish.

Cover the ham with the apple
slices and sprinkle them with the
spices. Pour the cider over the
apples, then cover the dish and
bake for about 1 hour. Remove
the lid for the last 10 minutes of
cooking time, and baste the ham
frequently with the juices.

BOILED BACON WITH CABBAGE

This is a classic combination of fine Irish ingredients. Serve with parsley sauce, which may be made with some of the water from the boiled cabbage.

Serves 6-8

INGREDIENTS
Collar or hock bacon joint,
  weighing about 1.4kg/3lbs
680-900g/1½-2lbs green cabbage
1 small onion
2-3 tbsps demerara sugar
Parsley sauce made with 570ml/1
  pint milk (see page 84)

Soak the bacon joint for 3-4 hours, then rinse and place in a pan of cold water. Bring slowly to the boil, skim away any scum, then simmer, allowing 20 minutes per 460g/1lb plus 20 minutes over.

Towards the end of cooking time, cut the cabbage in half, remove the thick stalk and cut the cabbage into quarters. Place in a large pan with the onion, cut in two; add 3-4 ladles of cooking liquor from the bacon and simmer the cabbage for 15 minutes. Remove the onion, drain the cabbage and chop it roughly with a metal spoon.

Remove the skin from the bacon, cut the fat into a pattern and coat it with brown sugar. Brown under a preheated grill or in a very hot oven.

Slice the bacon and serve with the cabbage and parsley sauce.

MARINATED PORK CHOPS

I always think that pork chops are much better value than lamb – and it is such a treat if you can get them with the kidney in.

Serves 4

INGREDIENTS
4 pork chops
1 tbsp freshly chopped mixed
   herbs, including sage and
   thyme
1 onion, finely chopped
430ml/¾ pint cider
60g/2oz seasoned flour
2 tbsps oil
15g/½oz butter
2 dessert apples, peeled, cored
   and sliced
1 tsp honey
1 tsp French mustard
150ml/¼ pint stock

Place the chops in a shallow ovenproof dish just large enough to hold them. Scatter the herbs and onion over the chops and add the cider. Leave for 2-3 hours, turning once or twice in the marinade.

Heat the oil and butter together in a frying pan. Drain the chops and dry them on absorbent kitchen paper, then toss them in the seasoned flour and brown on both sides. Strain the marinade into a bowl, then wash and butter the ovenproof dish. Lay the apples in the bottom and place the chops on top. Fry the onion from the marinade in the fat left in the pan, then stir in the remaining seasoned flour. Allow the roux to brown, stirring it constantly, then add the marinade and bring the sauce to the boil. Add the honey and mustard, then pour the sauce over the chops, cover the dish and bake for 45 minutes.

SAUSAGE & LENTILS

This is a good way of serving sausages – the lentils make a pleasant change from the usual accompaniment of mashed potatoes.

Serves 4

INGREDIENTS
1 onion
6 cloves
1.14 litres/2 pints water
Bouquet garni
225g/8oz red lentils
30g/1oz butter
Salt and freshly ground black
　pepper
8 thick pork sausages

Preheat an oven to 200°C/400°F/ Gas Mark 6. Stick the onion with the cloves, then place it in a pan with the water, bouquet garni and lentils. Bring to the boil, reduce the heat and simmer for 15 minutes. Remove the bouquet garni, drain the lentils and beat them into a paste with the butter; add salt and pepper to taste.

Make a bed of the lentils in an ovenproof serving dish, then arrange the sausages on top. Bake in the preheated oven for 30 minutes, until the sausages are browned, turning once during cooking.

SAUSAGE
TOAD-IN-THE-HOLE

Sausage toad is one of my favourite dishes – I like to serve it with baked beans and boiled cabbage.

Serves 6

INGREDIENTS
175g/6oz plain flour
Pinch of salt
2 eggs, size 3, beaten
570ml/1 pint milk, or milk and
    water mixed

2 tbsps oil
12 thick pork sausages
1 small onion, finely chopped

Preheat an oven to 220°C/425°F/Gas Mark 7. Mix the flour, salt and eggs together in a bowl, then gradually whisk in the milk. Leave the batter to stand for 10-15 minutes.

Place the oil and sausages in a roasting tin and bake in the hot oven for 10 minutes. Remove the tin and add the onion and the batter, then return the tin to the oven and cook for about 30 minutes, until the batter is browned and crisp. Serve immediately.

SAUSAGE PIE

There are many miles of beautiful coastline in Ireland, and plenty of secluded inland areas ideal for picnics. This is an easy dish to pack up and take with you.

Serves 6

INGREDIENTS

340g/12 oz prepared puff pastry
460g/1lb lean pork sausagemeat
1 small onion, very finely chopped
90g/3oz fresh white breadcrumbs
1 tsp dried sage
Salt and freshly ground black
    pepper
200g/7oz can chopped tomatoes
1 egg, size 3, beaten
1 tbsp milk

Preheat an oven to 200°C/400°F/ Gas Mark 6. Cut the pastry in two and roll out each piece to make a 25cm/10-inch circle. Use one piece to line a pie plate, and set the other aside in the fridge while preparing the filling.

Mix together the onion, breadcrumbs, sage, salt and pepper, then add the sausagemeat and tomatoes and the beaten egg. Spread the mixture over the pastry base on the pie plate, then cover with the remaining pastry, sealing and crimping the edges together.

Brush the pie with the milk and bake for 45 minutes.

POULTRY & GAME

Game was widely available and very popular in Ireland for many centuries. It provided food for both the rich and the poor and, certainly in country areas, there was always rabbit or pheasant available to make a meal.

Many cottagers kept poultry, often of several varieties. Hens, ducks and geese were common, guinea fowl were sometimes kept, and turkeys became popular after they were introduced to Ireland and the rest of Europe from America. Chickens were kept for their eggs and were boiled for meat only at the end of their productive life. Surplus eggs were sold at market and provided an income for country families. Pigeons were also kept for food, although all the pigeons eaten today are wild – given the natural scavenging abilities of the birds, it does seem unnecessary to go to the expense of feeding them when they can easily feed themselves.

Small Birds and Big Game

Puffin was also eaten, sometimes roasted on a spit over an open fire. These comical birds with their brightly coloured bills have such an endearing appeal for most of us that it is hard to imagine eating them, but they are still a popular food in countries such as Iceland, where they are plentiful. For many centuries eating was not subject to sentimentality, it was a matter of survival. It is only recently that factory farming and over-production have caused many people to lose respect for the animals that we eat and, at the same time, allowed sentimentality to colour our approach to food.

In addition to the game birds that we eat today, we can be certain that the Irish, in common with many other peoples of Europe, feasted off a variety of small birds such as thrushes, blackbirds and nightingales, as well as wild peacock and goose, plover and swan. Blackbirds were particularly important to the poor, who otherwise lived on a diet of salt herring – they provided a welcome contrast to the preserved fish. In wealthier households blackbirds were baked in pies – that isn't just a story in a nursery rhyme! Swan was not a common food, but was served at banquets and major festivals.

Wild game is still seasonally available in Ireland, but although there are plenty of pheasants, other birds such as partridge are now in relatively short supply. There are lots of rabbits and some hares, and venison is available both farmed and wild. The Normans introduced the fallow deer to Ireland to complement the already dwindling stocks of the native red deer – there are still some red deer in Ireland and they are much prized for the flavour of their meat.

There was a great tradition of hunting in Ireland and hunting parties were very much a part of the lavish life-style of the upper-classes in Victorian times. On such occasions the main meal of the day was often eaten in the early evening, about 5pm, and lasted for many hours. Thus, after a good Irish fry for breakfast, the huntsmen could ride for a day without the host and hostess having to arrange for a lunch at mid-day.

Chickens in Ireland are a truly domestic animal – in many instances living indoors with the family! Within living memory there are tales of hens hatching by the fire, and many Irish dressers actually had hatching coops in the bottom drawer, in much the same way as some modern kitchen dressers now have space for dog baskets in the bottom.

Free-range for Better Flavour

Poultry keeping was very much women's work and, in many cases, earned enough to pay the rent and buy groceries. However, the move away from a self-supporting life-style to a more urban existence has meant that mass-produced chicken and poultry are now the norm. The flavour and, in many cases, the quality of the birds has suffered as a consequence. In recent years there has been a move towards free-range poultry farming in Ireland, but whilst having a better flavour, the birds attract a premium price that many people are unwilling to pay.

The Michaelmas Goose

Geese have a comparatively short season, which begins on Michaelmas Day – the 29th of September. This was traditionally a rent day or hiring day and a tenant who had no money with which to pay the landlord would often offer a goose instead. Once the potato was an established crop in Ireland it was common for geese to be kept in a barn for the final fortnight of their lives, to be fed on a mash of milk and potatoes before being slaughtered. In areas such as Munster and south Ulster goose would be accompanied by baked apples and a glass of cider at Michaelmas, to mark the beginning of the apple harvest.

COLD CHICKEN IN TARRAGON SAUCE

This is a popular dish in Ireland – I first came across it when an Irish celebrity contributed it to a charity cookbook that I was editing. It is a perfect dish for summer entertaining.

Serves 6-8

INGREDIENTS
1.6kg/3½lb chicken
1 bay leaf
1 onion
1 carrot
1 stick celery
3 sprigs tarragon
Salt and white pepper

Sauce
60g/2oz butter
60g/2oz flour
150ml/¼ pint white wine or cider
90ml/3 fl oz double cream, whipped
3 tbsps mayonnaise
1 tbsp freshly chopped tarragon
1 tbsp freshly chopped parsley
Juice of ½ lemon

Place the chicken and bay leaf in a pan, add all the vegetables cut into quarters and the seasonings, then add sufficient cold water to just cover the chicken. Bring to the boil, then simmer for 1 hour, until the chicken is cooked. Leave the chicken to cool in the pan.

Melt the butter, stir in the flour then cook for 1 minute without allowing the roux to brown. Gradually stir in the wine, then add 280ml/½ pint of liquor from the chicken. Bring the sauce to the boil and simmer for 2-3 minutes, stirring constantly. Season lightly then leave to cool.

Remove the meat from the chicken and cut into bite-sized pieces. Add the remaining ingredients to the sauce and season to taste, then stir in the prepared chicken. Chill lightly before serving.

ROAST STUFFED CHICKEN

Chickens have traditionally been kept by country people the world over as they provide valuable eggs and are suitable for the pot once they have finished laying. Older chickens had to be boiled, so roast chicken was not a common dish until comparatively recently.

Serves 6

INGREDIENTS
1 small onion, finely chopped
90g/3oz fresh breadcrumbs
Grated rind and juice of 1 lemon
1 tbsp freshly chopped parsley
    and thyme
Salt and freshly ground black
    pepper
1 egg, size 3, beaten
1.6kg/3½lb chicken
30g/1oz butter, melted

Preheat an oven to 180°C/350°F/ Gas Mark 4. Combine the onion, breadcrumbs, lemon rind and juice, herbs and seasonings and bind the mixture together with the beaten egg. Add a little milk or water if the stuffing is too dry.

Remove any lumps of fat from the chicken cavity, then stuff the bird at the neck end – do not pack the stuffing in too tightly. Truss the chicken with string, then place it on a trivet in a roasting tin and brush with the melted butter. Cover with foil and roast for about 1¾ hours – the chicken is cooked if the juices run clear from the thickest part of the leg when the meat is pierced with a skewer. Remove the foil for the last 30 minutes of the cooking time and baste the bird before returning it to the oven.

Allow the chicken to stand for 10 minutes before carving.

CHICKEN, HAM & LEEK PIE

The addition of fresh cream and egg yolks at the end of cooking time gives this pie a typically Irish richness and flavour.

Serves 6-8

INGREDIENTS

1.14kg/3lb chicken
1 onion
1 bay leaf
Parsley stalks
Salt and freshly ground black pepper
460g/1lb leeks, cut into 4cm/1½-inch pieces
30g/1oz butter
1 tbsp freshly chopped parsley
120g/4oz cooked ham, diced
400g/14oz prepared puff pastry
1 egg, beaten
150ml/¼ pint double cream

Place the chicken in a saucepan with the onion and seasonings, cover with cold water and bring to the boil. Simmer slowly for 1 hour, or until the chicken is cooked, then leave it to cool in the pan. Cook the leeks in the butter for about 5 minutes, then leave until required.

Remove the meat from the carcass, cutting it into bite-sized pieces, and reserve the stock.

Combine the chicken, leeks, parsley and ham in a large pie dish with plenty of salt and pepper, then add 280ml/½ pint of the stock from the chicken.

Preheat an oven to 220°C/425°F/Gas Mark 7. Roll out the pastry and use it to cover the pie dish; use any trimmings to make pastry leaves for decoration. Make a slit in the pastry to allow the steam to escape then brush with beaten egg to glaze. Bake the pie for 15 minutes, then reduce the oven temperature to 200°C/400°F/Gas Mark 6 and cook for a further 20 minutes, until the pastry is well-risen and golden.

Warm the remaining egg and cream in a small pan. Remove one section of the pie crust then stir the mixture into the filling, replace the crust carefully and serve.

BOILED CHICKEN & PARSLEY SAUCE

Parsley sauce is a very traditional accompaniment to many meats in Ireland and was a popular way of dressing up a boiled chicken.

Serves 6

INGREDIENTS
45g/1½oz butter or lard
1 large boiling fowl
1 onion
1 carrot
1 turnip
1 stick celery
Bouquet garni
Salt and freshly ground black
   pepper
Parsley sauce (see recipe page 84)

Melt the fat in a pan just large enough to take the chicken, then add the prepared bird and brown it all over. Cut the vegetables into quarters, add them to the pan with the bouquet garni and seasonings, then add sufficient cold water to cover the chicken. Bring to the boil, then simmer the chicken for about 3 hours – allow 40 minutes per 460g/1lb.

Prepare a parsley sauce to serve with the chicken using 280ml/½ pint of milk and the same quantity of stock from the boiled chicken. Allow the chicken to stand for 10 minutes before carving or jointing and serve with the parsley sauce.

HOT TARRAGON CHICKEN

Chicken and tarragon make a perfect combination of flavours. This special dish is straightforward to prepare and should be served with fresh soda bread or potatoes and a green salad.

Serves 4

INGREDIENTS

60g/2oz butter
4 boneless chicken breasts, skinned
2 tbsps fresh tarragon
150ml/¼ pint white wine
150ml/¼ pint double cream
Salt and freshly ground black pepper

Melt the butter in a large frying-pan and brown the chicken breasts on both sides, then cook them slowly for about 8 minutes, until cooked through. Keep the chicken warm on a serving plate while preparing the sauce.

Add the wine and tarragon to the pan juices and boil rapidly until slightly reduced, scraping up any sediment from the bottom of the pan. Reduce the heat and add the cream, then bring gently to the boil. Season the sauce to taste, return the chicken to the pan and reheat for 1-2 minutes before serving.

BRAISED CHICKEN

Chickens that are to be braised are usually jointed, but a whole chicken can also be cooked in this way. Rather than stuffing the bird, I would suggest placing a whole lemon in the cavity – stuffings tend to become soggy in a braised bird.

Serves 4-6

INGREDIENTS

1 onion, sliced
1 carrot, sliced
4 rashers streaky bacon, rinded
  and chopped
1 lemon
1.8kg/4lb chicken
1 tbsp freshly chopped herbs
12 black peppercorns
6 cloves
3 bay leaves
Salt and freshly ground black
  pepper
570ml/1 pint stock or water
30g/1oz butter
30g/1oz flour

Place the prepared vegetables and bacon in the bottom of a pan just large enough to take the chicken. Scrub the lemon, pierce it a few times with a fork then place it in the cavity of the chicken and lay the bird on the bed of vegetables.

Add the seasonings and stock to the pan, then cover the chicken with a double layer of greased greaseproof paper or a butter paper. Simmer for 2 hours, basting the chicken occasionally over the paper. The chicken may be browned in a very hot oven before serving, if desired.

Remove the chicken from the pan and keep it warm. Work the butter and flour together, then strain the stock and return it to the pan. Reheat the stock, then thicken it by adding the butter and flour mixture gradually, beating well and boiling after each addition. Season the sauce to taste, then serve the chicken with the sauce poured over. The vegetables may be served with the chicken or made into soup.

CHICKEN GALANTINE

This is a traditional way of preparing a galantine. A chicken galantine makes a wonderful centrepiece for a cold buffet and was a popular dish for country house entertaining.

Serves 6-8

INGREDIENTS
1.4kg/3lb chicken, boned
225g/8oz ham, minced
225g/8oz sausagemeat
1 tbsp freshly chopped mixed herbs
Salt and freshly ground black pepper
1 egg, size 3, beaten
280ml/½ pint chicken stock
1 stick celery, sliced
2 carrots, sliced
2 onions, sliced
6 peppercorns
Fresh herbs to garnish
1 tsp gelatine

Carefully remove all the meat from the chicken carcass and cut it into slices. Butter a muslin cloth and arrange half the chicken in a layer on it. Combine the ham, sausagemeat, herbs, seasonings and egg and spread the mixture over the chicken, then top with the remaining meat slices – you may make more layers if you wish, but start and finish with a layer of chicken.

Roll up the cloth and tie it securely to keep the galantine in shape. Place in a pan with the stock and prepared vegetables; bring to the boil, then simmer gently for 3 hours.

Remove the galantine from the pan in the cloth and allow it to cool. Remove the cloth and transfer the meat to a serving dish. Garnish the meat with sprigs of fresh herbs. Strain the stock, sprinkle the gelatine over it and stir until completely dissolved. Reheat the stock gently to dissolve the gelatine if necessary, but do not allow it to boil. Allow the glaze to cool, then spoon it, a little at a time, over the galantine, chilling each layer. Continue glazing until there is a reasonable layer of jelly over the chicken. Chill thoroughly and serve sliced.

This galantine could also be made in a pudding basin and steamed if a muslin cloth is not available, although the galantine may then be a little drier.

QUAILS À LA POLONAISE

Wild quail are rare now in Ireland, but quail farming is being developed and several supermarkets now stock oven-ready birds. This traditional recipe uses finely chopped hard-boiled egg as a coating.

Serves 2

INGREDIENTS
4 prepared quails
Salt and freshly ground black
  pepper
60g/2oz butter, melted
1 hard-boiled egg, very finely
  chopped
30g/1oz fresh breadcrumbs
1 tbsp freshly chopped parsley
1 lemon, cut into quarters
Watercress to garnish

Split the quail down the breastbone and flatten each one out in one piece. Place breast side down in a shallow, ovenproof dish, season well and brush with a little melted butter. Mix the egg with the breadcrumbs and parsley.

Preheat the grill and cook the quails until golden brown, then turn the birds over and brush again with melted butter before grilling the second side. Spread the crumb mixture over the cooked quail, sprinkle the remaining butter over and grill again until the coating is crisp and lightly brown – take care as it can burn quite easily. Garnish with lemon quarters and watercress and serve immediately.

PIGEON PIE

*Pigeons are plentiful in Ireland if slightly out of fashion.
Pigeon pie was once very popular and it deserves to be so
again. Use only the breasts – the remaining meat may be
made into soup. The sausagemeat helps to keep the
pigeon moist.*

Serves 4

INGREDIENTS
4-6 pigeon breasts
45g/1½oz butter
225g/8oz sausagemeat, shaped
  into 8 balls
2 sticks celery, chopped
1 carrot, sliced
2 large onions, chopped
Salt and freshly ground black
  pepper
225g/8oz mushrooms, sliced
225ml/8 fl oz cider
2 tbsps freshly chopped mixed
  herbs
2 bay leaves
340g/12oz prepared shortcrust or
  puff pastry

Preheat an oven to 200°C/400°F/
Gas Mark 6. Cut the pigeon
breasts in half then brown them

well in the butter and place in a
large pie dish with the
sausagemeat balls. Add the celery,
carrot and onion to the pan juices
and cook until soft, then season
lightly and add the mushrooms.
Continue cooking for 2-3 minutes,
then add the cider and boil until
the sauce is slightly reduced. Add
the herbs and bay leaves, then
season to taste before pouring the
mixture over the pigeon breasts.

Roll out the prepared pastry and
use to cover the pie dish, placing
a pie funnel in the centre of the
dish to support the pastry crust.
Use any trimmings to decorate
the pie, then bake for 30-40
minutes until golden brown.

ROAST DUCK WITH ORANGE SAUCE

Duck used to be a very popular food in Ireland, and ponds which encouraged them were common in farmyards. It is less popular since chicken has become widely available at very competitive prices, but a wild duck is now a real treat. You may prefer to serve a traditional sage and onion stuffing with the duck in place of the orange sauce.

Serves 2-3

INGREDIENTS
1 oven-ready duck, weighing
   900g-1.14kg/2-3lbs
4 rashers streaky bacon, rinded

Sauce
1 orange
120ml/4 fl oz olive oil
1 tbsp white wine or tarragon
   vinegar
1 tsp caster sugar
Pinch of dry mustard
1 tsp freshly chopped tarragon
Salt and freshly ground black
   pepper

Preheat an oven to 230°C/450°F/Gas Mark 8. Cover the breast of the duck with the bacon, then place the bird on a trivet in a roasting tin and cook for 50 minutes – add an extra 10 minutes for every 225g/8oz over 900g/2lbs.

Prepare the orange sauce while the duck is cooking. Grate the rind from the orange or remove it with a zester, then peel the fruit. Slice the orange into rings, removing as many pips as possible. Combine all the remaining ingredients for the sauce, shaking them together in a jar, or whisking them thoroughly. Pour the dressing over the orange slices and zest and leave to marinate until the duck is ready to serve.

Stand the duck for 10 minutes before carving and serving with the sauce.

DUCKLING RINEANNA

This is a contemporary Irish dish based on a recipe created by Chef Ryan at the Shannon Airport restaurant.

Serves 4

INGREDIENTS
10 large dessert apples, Granny Smith's or Golden Delicious
60g/2oz butter
280ml/½ pint cider
Salt and freshly ground black pepper
1 tsp freshly chopped parsley
1 tsp freshly chopped fennel
Pinch of grated nutmeg
120g/4oz fresh breadcrumbs
1.8kg/4lb duckling
1 tsp flour
1 tbsp lemon juice
280ml/½ pint chicken stock
2 tsps arrowroot
½ tsp freshly chopped mint

Preheat an oven to 230°C/450°F/Gas Mark 8. Peel, core and quarter four of the apples, then cook them in the butter until just tender. Add half the cider and cook for a further 10 minutes. Season with salt, pepper, parsley, fennel and nutmeg, then add the breadcrumbs to give a firm but moist stuffing – you may not need quite all the breadcrumbs, depending on the size of the apples.

Stuff the duckling with the apple mixture and place it on a trivet in a roasting tin. Dredge the breast lightly with the flour, then roast the duck for 40-45 minutes. Peel and core the remaining apples, cut them into thick rings, then brush them with lemon juice. Poach the apple rings slowly in the stock until just tender – do not overcook them as they need to keep their shape as a garnish. Keep the duck warm while making the sauce.

Strain off any excess fat from the roasting tin, add the remaining cider and boil until the mixture is reduced by half. Dissolve the arrowroot in a little water, stir into the pan and continue stirring until the sauce has boiled and thickened. Season to taste and add the mint.

Serve the duckling garnished with the apple rings and with the sauce poured over.

ROAST TURKEY WITH CELERY SAUCE

A turkey is a good choice for a celebratory meal as it will serve many people. I always like to ensure that everyone gets a little of the dark meat as well as the white for a variety of flavours. Turkeys have been eaten in Ireland since the 18th century and are often served with a celery sauce, especially at Christmas.

Serves 10-12

INGREDIENTS

1 oven-ready turkey, about
    4.6kg/10lb in weight
900g/2lb pork sausagemeat
Salt and freshly ground black
    pepper
4 rashers back bacon

Sauce

1 head celery, trimmed, washed
    and chopped
280ml/½ pint chicken stock
60g/2oz butter
60g/2oz flour
570ml/1 pint milk
Freshly grated nutmeg
3-4 tbsps cream

Preheat an oven to 160°C/325°F/ Gas Mark 3. Prepare the turkey, stuff it with the sausagemeat and place it on its breast on a trivet in a roasting tin. Season lightly and cover with greaseproof paper or a butter paper. Roast for 2 hours, then turn the turkey over. Season the breast and cover with the bacon; cover with the butter paper and roast for a further 2 hours. The paper and bacon may be removed 30 minutes before the end of the cooking time to allow the breast to brown all over.

Place the celery in a pan with the stock and a little seasoning and simmer gently for 20-30 minutes until tender. Blend to a smooth purée in a liquidiser or food processor. Melt the butter in a pan, stir in the flour and cook for 1 minute without browning. Gradually add the milk off the heat then bring the sauce to the boil, stirring all the time. Add the celery purée, then season to taste with salt, pepper and nutmeg. Reheat the sauce as necessary to accompany the turkey, adding the cream just before serving.

ROAST GOOSE WITH POTATO STUFFING

Goose was the traditional food for festive occasions in Ireland – it was often boiled or braised in homes where there was no oven, but roasting is by far the most popular method of cooking. The unusual potato stuffing helps to absorb any greasiness from the goose.

Serves 6

INGREDIENTS
225g/8oz streaky bacon, rinded and chopped
2 onions, finely chopped
1 small head celery, trimmed and chopped
900g/2lbs cooked mashed potatoes
120g/4oz butter
225ml/8 fl oz milk
3 tbsps freshly chopped mixed herbs
Salt and freshly ground black pepper
1 goose, about 4.6kg/10lbs prepared weight

Preheat an oven to 160°C/325°F/ Gas Mark 3. Fry the bacon until crisp, then add the onions and celery and cook until just softened. Mix all the remaining ingredients together and add the bacon mixture, then use to stuff the goose.

Prick the skin of the goose all over and truss the bird. Place on a trivet in a roasting tin, breast side down, and cook for about 3½ hours. Turn the goose over half-way through cooking. Stand the goose for 10-15 minutes before carving and serve with apple sauce and gravy.

PHEASANT BRAISED IN RED WINE

This is a traditional recipe for a casserole, and an excellent method of cooking pheasant, as any but the best birds can be rather dry when roasted.

Serves 4

INGREDIENTS
2 tbsps oil
15g/½oz butter
1 large pheasant
2 dessert apples, cored and
    quartered, but not peeled
1 onion, chopped
1 tbsp seasoned flour
150ml/¼ pint red wine
150ml/¼ pint stock
Grated rind and juice of 1 orange
Bouquet garni
1 tsp demerara sugar
Salt and freshly ground black
    pepper

Preheat an oven to 180°C/350°F/ Gas Mark 4. Heat the oil and butter together in a large pan and brown the pheasant on all sides, then transfer the bird to a casserole dish with the apples. Cook the onion until soft in the fat left in the pan, then stir in the flour and cook for 1 minute. Gradually add the wine and stock off the heat, then bring to the boil, stirring all the time. Add the orange rind and juice, the bouquet garni and sugar; season to taste with salt and pepper.

Pour the sauce over the pheasant, then cover and cook for 1 hour. Serve carved or jointed.

PARTRIDGE CASSEROLE

Partridges are now quite rare in Ireland. They were often kept just for the gentry and in many country houses they were used as a filling for stuffed vine leaves. This is a far more straightforward recipe.

Serves 2

INGREDIENTS

30g/1oz lard or dripping
120g/4oz bacon, diced
2 young partridges, halved
1 tbsp seasoned flour
1 small onion, finely chopped
1 carrot, sliced
2 sticks celery, sliced
1 cooking apple, peeled, cored
  and sliced
15g/½oz flour
175ml/6 fl oz white wine or cider
175ml/6 fl oz game stock
2 stalks parsley
1 sprig thyme
1 sprig marjoram
Salt and freshly ground black
  pepper
90g/3oz seedless raisins
150ml/¼ pint single cream

Heat the lard in a heavy-based pan and brown the bacon, then remove it with a slotted spoon. Dredge the birds with the seasoned flour and brown them in the bacon fat, then remove from the pan. Toss the vegetables and the apple slices in the fat, cook for 5 minutes and stir in the flour. Gradually add the wine and stock, then bring the sauce to the boil and add the herbs and raisins.

Return the partridge pieces and the bacon to the pan; cover and simmer slowly for 25-30 minutes, until the partridge is tender. Remove the partridge to a warmed serving plate, then boil the sauce to reduce it slightly, if necessary. Season to taste, remove the sprigs of herbs and stir in the cream. Serve the sauce poured over the partridge.

ROAST PHEASANT

Always choose young pheasants for roasting or the meat may be dry. Hanging the bird helps tenderise the meat and gives it a stronger, more gamy flavour.

Serves 4

INGREDIENTS
2 young hen pheasants
4 rashers streaky bacon, rinded
60g/2oz butter, softened
150ml/¼ pint stock
150ml/¼ pint red wine or port
2 tbsps redcurrant jelly
30g/1oz fresh breadcrumbs
Watercress for garnish

Stuffing
45g/1½oz butter
1 small onion, finely chopped
1 cooking apple, peeled and
    grated
Juice of ½ lemon
Salt and freshly ground black
    pepper

Game chips
3-4 potatoes
Oil for deep-frying
Salt

Preheat an oven to 190°C/375°F/ Gas Mark 5. Melt 15g/½oz butter for the stuffing and cook the onion until soft and transparent. Toss the grated apple in lemon juice, add the onion and butter, season well and mix; divide the stuffing between the cavities of the prepared pheasants. Truss the birds, and arrange the bacon over their breasts, seasoning well with black pepper. Smear the pheasants with softened butter, then place them on a trivet in a roasting tin and cook for about 1 hour, basting frequently. The pheasants are cooked if the juices run clear when the thigh is pierced with a skewer – do not overcook or the pheasants will be tough.

Prepare the game chips while the pheasants are roasting. Peel the potatoes and slice them very thinly. Rinse in cold water and pat dry on absorbent kitchen paper.

Deep-fry the potatoes in hot oil for about 3 minutes – cook in batches and allow the oil to regain its heat between each batch. The chips should be fried again for 1-2 minutes just before serving, and sprinkled with salt.

Remove the bacon and string from the pheasants then allow them to stand for 10 minutes. Strain off any surplus fat from the meat juices, then add the stock and wine or port and simmer until slightly reduced, stirring up all the sediment from the bottom of the pan. Add the redcurrant jelly and breadcrumbs, season to taste then serve with the pheasant.

ROAST SADDLE OF VENISON WITH SPICED PEARS

Venison is once again growing in popularity, and with deer now being farmed for meat, it is also becoming more affordable. The saddle is the traditional roasting joint and benefits from being cooked rare. Marinating helps the meat develop its full gamy flavour.

Serves 8-10

INGREDIENTS
Marinade
280ml/½ pint olive oil
280ml/½ pint red wine vinegar
570ml/1 pint red wine
Bouquet garni
4 stalks parsley
Grated rind of ½ orange
8 juniper berries, crushed
1 onion, sliced
1 stick celery, sliced
1 clove garlic, crushed

1 saddle of venison, weighing
    about 2.7kg/6lbs
60g/2oz butter, softened
Salt and freshly ground black
    pepper
4-5 ripe pears (allow ½ a pear per
    person)
2 tsps ground cinnamon

Mix all the marinade ingredients together and pour over the venison in a large dish. Cover and leave for 2 days in a cool larder or the refrigerator, turning the venison in the marinade from time to time.

Preheat an oven to 190°C/375°F/ Gas Mark 5. Remove the venison from the marinade and pat dry on absorbent kitchen paper. Transfer the venison to a roasting tin and smear the meat with half the butter, then season well with salt and pepper. Cover with foil and roast for 1½-2 hours, basting frequently. Allow 10-15 minutes per 460g/1lb for rare meat and 13-18 for medium.

Half-an-hour before the end of cooking, peel the pears and cut them in half. Dot with the remaining butter and sprinkle with cinnamon then add them to the roasting tin and baste them with the juices. Remove the foil from the venison 10 minutes before the end of cooking and raise the oven temperature to 200°C/400°F/Gas Mark 6 to brown both the meat and the pears.

Stand the meat for 5-10 minutes before carving. Take the fillets from the backbone, then cut long slices from the length of the joint. Serve with the spiced pears.

RABBIT IN MUSTARD SAUCE

Rabbit has been a popular food for many centuries in Ireland – they are thought to have been introduced to the British Isles by the Romans. Rabbits were easily available to country folk – the young ones were called graziers and were often roasted, casseroled or boiled.

Serves 4

INGREDIENTS
1.8kg/4lb rabbit, cleaned and jointed
4 tbsps mild mustard
30g/1oz butter
15g/½oz dripping or lard
1 onion, finely chopped
30g/1oz flour
430ml/¾ pint dry cider or white wine
2 sprigs fresh thyme
1 sprig fresh rosemary
Salt and freshly ground black pepper

Smear the rabbit pieces with the mustard and leave them for 2-3 hours to absorb the flavour.

Melt the butter and dripping together in a large frying-pan and fry the rabbit pieces until golden brown. Remove the rabbit with a slotted spoon, then add the onion to the pan and cook until soft. Stir in the flour and cook for 1 minute. Gradually add the cider, off the heat, then stir in the herbs and bring the sauce slowly to the boil, stirring all the time. Season lightly, then return the rabbit to the pan; cover and simmer slowly for 45-60 minutes, or until tender.

BRAISED RABBIT

This is a rich, gamy casserole that can traditionally be made with rabbit or hare – I prefer the flavour of rabbit.

Serves 4

INGREDIENTS
120g/4oz cooked rice
120g/4oz mushrooms, chopped
120g/4oz sausagemeat
1 onion, finely chopped
Salt and freshly ground black
  pepper
2 eggs, size 3, beaten
1 rabbit
1 tbsp seasoned flour
15g/½oz butter
1 tbsp olive oil
280ml/½ pint brown stock
120ml/4 fl oz red wine

Combine the rice, mushrooms, sausagemeat and onion; season well, then bind the stuffing mixture with the beaten eggs. Use the mixture to stuff the rabbit, shaping any stuffing that is left over into balls.

Dredge the rabbit with the seasoned flour, then brown it in the butter and oil in a large frying-pan. Add the stock and wine, then cover and simmer for 1 hour. Add any balls of left-over stuffing and simmer the rabbit for a further 30 minutes, until tender.

JUGGED HARE

*Hares used to be plentiful in Ireland, but they are becoming
increasingly difficult to find in the wild. You will probably
need to order a hare from your butcher for this recipe – ask
for a young leveret and be sure to ask for the 'pot' or blood
to be kept if you want to use it to thicken the sauce.*

Serves 4

INGREDIENTS

1 young hare or large rabbit,
   jointed
60g/2oz seasoned flour
90g/3oz butter or dripping
280ml/½ pint stock
150ml/¼ pint red wine
1 onion
8 cloves
Grated rind of ½ lemon
1 blade mace
Bouquet garni
Salt and freshly ground black
   pepper

Toss the joints in the seasoned
flour, then brown them quickly in
60g/2oz of the butter. Remove the
hare from the pan with a slotted
spoon, then stir any remaining
flour into the pan juices and cook
until it is browned. Add the stock
and wine off the heat, then
gradually bring the sauce to the
boil, stirring all the time.

Return the hare to the pan with
the onion stuck with the cloves
and the remaining seasonings.
Cover and simmer, allowing about
1½ hours for rabbit and 2-3 hours
for hare. Remove the hare to a
warmed serving plate, then strain
the sauce, season and serve
poured over the meat. The blood
may be added to the casserole for
the final 15 minutes of cooking,
but the hare should be simmered
very slowly after the blood has
been added and should not be
boiled.

SWEETS & DESSERTS

Old habits die hard in Ireland, and many daily activities continue in much the same way as they have done for centuries. Thus the pattern of eating remains much as it has always been and there are many people in Ireland who would not leave the dining table without having had a pudding to conclude their meal. This need not be grand, complicated or fussy, but it should certainly be there.

Wild Fruits and Honey

In the very earliest days of recorded Irish culinary history the most common dessert was fruit served with honey. Many fruits grew wild, but others, such as apples, have been cultivated since before the Normans landed in the 12th century. The Normans brought a variety of new foods and ideas with them and generally started to organise the agricultural system in Ireland. The most common wild fruits were berries – raspberries, blackberries, strawberries, elderberries and bilberries – but sloes and crab apples were also plentiful. Honey was commonly used as a sweetener, and although sugar was known, it did not come into common use until the 17th century. Nuts were also mixed with fruits to serve as puddings and the native hazelnut was widely acclaimed, along with walnuts and filberts. Almonds became very popular as a flavouring for tarts and cakes, but they were introduced by the French and were far more expensive than the native varieties of nut.

French Skills for Pies and Tarts

In keeping with their great tradition of bread baking, the Irish are also great pastry cooks. The art of pastry making seems to have been learnt from the early Norman settlers, so it was not long before fruits were being made into pies and tarts and baked in ovens constructed from an upturned pot placed in the ashes of a fire. The Normans established formal apple orchards in the southeastern counties of Ireland, in Armagh, Down and Fermanagh, and these places remain amongst the top apple-producing areas in Ireland today.

Although the Irish tend towards a sweet tooth and will devote much time and energy to the making and decoration of delicious and elaborate desserts, throughout history many of their puddings have been simple and wholesome – an effective way of filling hungry stomachs at very little cost. Filling suet puddings have always been popular, packed either with dried fruits or fresh fruits in season. Such puddings were cheap to make and easy to cook, simply requiring a long, slow steam over the fire. The very simple recipe for a fresh fruit plum pudding in this chapter is one of my favourites – a simple celebration of traditional foods.

Milk and Cream in Many Desserts

Milk and cream of the highest quality are plentiful in Ireland, and so it is inevitable that both these ingredients should play a very important part in the traditional pudding recipes of the country. Oats were often mixed with milk and cream to make gruels of varying consistencies – thin would be for breakfast, but a thicker version, sometimes made with cream rather than milk and sweetened with honey, was served as a dessert. This was the start of flummery, a most delicious pudding to which I often add whiskey and stewed fruits. Baked custards were widely made, again to be served with fresh or died fruits, and stale bread or scraps from a loaf were soaked in milk before being beaten with dried fruits and made into bread pudding. Milk and cream were also simmered with carrageen, gathered from the beaches, until the natural jelly flowed from the seaweed giving a setting agent for milk jellies. Such jellies are delicious when served with plenty of sauce made from cream or sieved soft cheese, whiskey and honey.

The Mayday Blancmange

Milk was also frequently made into blancmange, thickened with flour and set as a simple but nutritious dessert. There were great tales associated with blancmanges made for Mayday, officially the first day of summer in Ireland. If there was enough flour left from the winter stores of wheat to make a blancmange on Mayday, it proved the housekeeping skills of the maker who had successfully ensured that the stores gathered in the autumn had lasted right through the long winter months.

CARRAGEEN MOSS PUDDING

Carrageen grows on the Atlantic coast, not only in Ireland but also in Wales and Scotland. It makes a nutritious milk jelly pudding – I like to serve it with a creamy whiskey sauce!

Serves 4

INGREDIENTS
8g/¼oz dried carrageen moss
570ml/1 pint milk
Grated rind of ½ lemon
30g/1oz caster sugar

It is difficult to weigh such a small amount of carrageen, so a good measure is to use as much as will fit into your clenched fist. Wash the moss, then place it in a pan with the remaining ingredients and bring slowly to the boil. Simmer gently for 15-20 minutes – you should see the moss begin to ooze a thick jelly.

Strain the mixture through a sieve, pressing all the jelly through and scraping it from the bottom of the sieve. Stir well, then turn the mixture into a serving bowl or a mould which has been rinsed with cold water. Leave to set in the refrigerator for 3-4 hours or overnight, then turn out onto a serving plate. Moss pudding is traditionally served with cream and strawberry or raspberry jam.

IRISH COFFEE CAKE

This is the ideal way to transform a perfectly ordinary sponge cake into a deliciously decadent dessert, simply by adding the ingredients for an Irish coffee: cream, coffee and whiskey.

Serves 8

INGREDIENTS
120g/4oz butter
120g/4oz caster sugar
120g/4oz self-raising flour
Pinch of salt
2 tsps instant coffee
2 tbsps hot water
2 eggs, size 3, beaten

Syrup
150ml/¼ pint strong coffee
120g/4oz caster sugar
3 tbsps Irish whiskey

Topping
1 tbsp icing sugar, sieved
1 tbsp Irish whiskey
150ml/¼ pint double cream, whipped
Chopped hazelnuts for decoration

Preheat an oven to 180°C/350°F/Gas Mark 4, then butter a 20cm/8-inch ring tin and flour it lightly.

Cream the butter and sugar until light and fluffy, then add the eggs, one at a time. Sieve the flour and salt and fold two-thirds into the creamed butter. Dissolve the coffee in the water, then add it to the mixture followed by the remaining flour. Spoon into the prepared tin and smooth the top, then bake for 35-40 minutes until just starting to shrink from the sides of the tin. Carefully turn the cake out onto a wire rack to cool.

To make the syrup, heat the coffee and sugar gently until the sugar has dissolved, then boil rapidly for 1 minute. Remove the pan from the heat and stir in the whiskey. Wash the ring tin and return the cooled cake to it, then pour the syrup over the cake and leave it to soak for 2-3 hours.

Add the icing sugar and whiskey to the whipped cream. Turn the cake out onto a serving plate and decorate with the whipped cream and chopped hazelnuts. Chill well before serving.

FLUMMERY

Flummery is an ancient Celtic dish based on traditional recipes for oatmeal gruel. The oatmeal is toasted in this recipe and then folded into a base of whipped cream.

Serves 4

INGREDIENTS
60g/2oz slivered almonds
60g/2oz medium oatmeal
280ml/½ pint double or whipping
   cream
3-4 tbsps honey
1-2 tsps lemon juice

Toast the almonds and oatmeal in a heavy-based pan until golden brown, then allow to cool completely. Whisk the cream until thick but not stiff, then fold in the honey and lemon juice – a tablespoon or so of whiskey or liqueur may be added at this stage. Fold in the almond and oatmeal mixture, then spoon the flummery into individual dishes and chill before serving.

TIPSY CAKE

*This might well be called a trifle, but to the Irish it is very
definitely Tipsy Cake.*

Serves 8

INGREDIENTS
400g/14oz can fruit cocktail
60ml/2 fl oz whiskey or sherry
6 trifle sponges
Raspberry jam
60g/2oz ratafia biscuits, crushed
60g/2oz flaked almonds

Custard
2 tbsps cornflour
30g/1oz vanilla or caster sugar
Vanilla essence (optional)
280ml/½ pint milk
1 tbsp whiskey or sherry
1 egg, size 3, beaten

280ml/½ pint double cream,
  whipped
Glacé cherries to decorate

Drain the fruit into a bowl, then measure out 60ml/2 fl oz of the syrup and add the whiskey or sherry. Slice the trifle sponges in half and spread them lightly with raspberry jam, then cut diagonally and place a layer of sponge in the bottom of a glass bowl. Top with half the fruit, some of the ratafias and flaked almonds, then pour a little of the fortified juice over the mixture. Repeat the layers with the remaining sponges, fruit and almonds, finishing with a layer of sponge, then pour the remaining juice over the trifle base. Reserve the remaining crushed ratafias to decorate the finished dish.

Mix the cornflour and sugar together in a bowl and add the vanilla essence, if using plain sugar. Blend to a paste with a little of the cold milk, then bring the rest of the milk to the boil. Pour it over the cornflour mixture, stirring all the time, then return the custard to the rinsed-out pan, bring to the boil and simmer for 1 minute, stirring all the time. Allow the custard to cool slightly, then beat in the whiskey or sherry and the egg. Pour the cooled custard over the trifle base and leave until completely cold.

Top with the whipped cream, then decorate with some quartered glacé cherries and the remaining ratafias. Chill before serving.

BANANAS WITH IRISH MIST

A delicious dessert flavoured with Irish Mist liqueur.

Serves 4

INGREDIENTS
4 large bananas
60g/2oz butter
1 tbsp caster sugar
1-2 tbsps Irish Mist liqueur

Melt the butter in a heavy-based frying-pan then add the peeled bananas and cook them in the melted butter for about 6 minutes, turning them over carefully half way through cooking. Keep the bananas warm on individual plates while making the sauce.

Add the sugar to the remaining butter in the pan and heat slowly until dissolved, then stir in the Irish Mist. Bring to the boil, then spoon the sauce over the hot bananas and serve immediately.

APPLE FOOL

This is a light, summery dessert, ideal for celebrating the start of the apple harvest in September.

Serves 4

INGREDIENTS
280ml/½ pint apple purée
Sugar to taste
150ml/¼ pint double cream, whipped
Mint leaves for decoration (optional)

Beat the apple purée until smooth, then sweeten it to taste with sugar. Fold in the whipped cream, then divide the fool between individual dishes and chill well. Decorate each portion with a small sprig of mint before serving.

Stewed rhubarb also makes a good base for a fool – make a purée from the cooked fruit and proceed as above.

BAKED APPLE DUMPLINGS

*Apple dumplings are so delicious when made with light,
buttery pastry – they certainly shouldn't be stodgy or heavy.*

Serves 6

INGREDIENTS

340g/12oz plain flour
¼ tsp salt
¼ tsp ground cinnamon
¼ tsp ground nutmeg
175g/6oz butter, cut into small
  pieces
Iced water to mix
6 medium-sized dessert apples,
  e.g. Granny Smith's
6 prunes, soaked and pitted
6 ready-to-eat dried apricots
2 tbsps seedless raisins
1 egg, size 3, beaten
Caster sugar

Preheat an oven to 160°C/325°F/
Gas Mark 3. Sieve the flour, salt
and spices together into a large
bowl, then rub into the butter
until the mixture resembles fine
breadcrumbs. Mix to a firm but
manageable dough with iced
water, then divide into 6 pieces.

Knead lightly and roll out into
20cm/8-inch squares.

Peel the apples and remove the
centres with a corer. Chop the
prunes and apricots and mix them
with the raisins, then use the
dried fruits to stuff the apples,
placing each one in the centre of
a square of pastry.

Brush the edges of the pastry with
water, then gather the dough up
around the apples, pinching it
together and sealing it at the top.
Any trimmings may be made into
pastry leaves for decoration. Place
the apples on a lightly buttered
baking sheet and brush with the
beaten egg. Sprinkle with a little
caster sugar, then bake for 20-25
minutes, until the pastry is golden
brown. Serve with cream, custard
or vanilla ice cream.

ALMOND TARTLETS

This recipe came from the Ballymaloe Hotel in County Cork, which is famed for its desserts.

Serves 6

INGREDIENTS
90g/3oz butter
90g/3oz caster sugar
90g/3oz ground almonds
120g/4oz raspberries
Whipped cream for decoration

Preheat an oven to 180°C/350°F/ Gas Mark 4 and lightly butter a tray of 12 patty tins.

Beat the butter, sugar and almonds together until creamy, then divide the mixture between the patty tins. Bake for 10-12 minutes, or until golden brown. Allow to cool slightly in the tins for 2-3 minutes, but transfer the tartlets to a cooling rack before they become hard. Decorate with raspberries, or other soft fruits in season, and whipped cream just before serving.

CREAMY RICE PUDDING

Modern convenience rice puddings in cans are a world apart from a rice pudding baked at home. This is the perfect dish for a cold winter's day.

Serves 4-6

INGREDIENTS
120g/4oz short-grain pudding rice
90g/3oz sugar
45g/1½oz butter, cut into slivers
1.14 litres/2 pints milk
Freshly grated nutmeg

Preheat an oven to 180°C/350°F/ Gas Mark 4. Wash the rice in a sieve, then place it in a large ovenproof casserole dish with the sugar and butter. Heat the milk until almost boiling, then pour it over the rice; grate plenty of nutmeg over the surface of the pudding. Bake for about 1½ hours, until thick and creamy. Serve with stewed fruit or jam.

SCRAP BREAD PUDDING

A well-made bread pudding with top quality fruits is a delight. Some people remove the crusts from the bread, but I do not think that it is necessary – once they are soaked they become soft enough to blend into the mixture.

Serves 6-8

INGREDIENTS
225g/8oz scrap bread
280ml/½ pint milk
30g/1oz flour
1 tsp baking powder
1-2 tsps mixed spice
Grated rind of 1 lemon
60g/2oz suet
60g/2oz currants
60g/2oz raisins
60g/2oz sultanas
30g/1oz chopped mixed peel
60g/2oz demerara sugar
1 egg, size 3, beaten
Demerara sugar for dredging

Preheat an oven to 180°C/350°F/ Gas Mark 4. Soak the bread in the milk for 30 minutes, then beat it thoroughly to remove any lumps – I sometimes use a potato masher on the bread to start this process. Sieve the flour, baking powder and spice into the mixture, then add all the remaining ingredients and mix well.

Turn the mixture into a buttered 20cm/8-inch flan dish, sandwich tin or similar and bake for 1-1¼ hours, until set. Scatter with a little extra demerara sugar as soon as the pudding comes out of the oven, then leave to cool in the tin before cutting into squares or wedges.

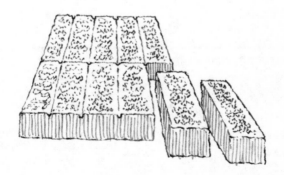

BREAD & BUTTER
PUDDING

This recipe has been adapted in recent years to include croissants, French bread and even fruit breads such as barm brack. I think this traditional version remains the best.

Serves 6

INGREDIENTS
4-5 slices bread
Butter for spreading
30g/3oz caster sugar
1 tsp ground cinnamon
60g/2oz sultanas
570ml/1 pint milk
2 eggs, size 3, beaten
Caster sugar for dredging

Preheat an oven to 180°C/350°F/ Gas Mark 4 and lightly butter a 1- litre/1¾-pint pie dish.

Butter the bread and cut it into triangles. Mix the sugar and cinnamon together, then layer the bread with the sugar and fruit in the dish, finishing with a layer of bread. Bring the milk almost to the boil, then pour it over the beaten eggs. Pour the custard over the bread, then bake the pudding for 40-45 minutes, until set. Dredge the pudding with a little extra sugar as soon as it comes out of the oven. Serve warm.

ALMOND PUDDING

Almonds are used extensively in sweet dishes but also in soups, especially with watercress. This recipe calls for grated marzipan, so leave the correct amount uncovered in the refrigerator for 2-3 hours before preparing the tart, so that it hardens and is easy to grate.

Serves 8

INGREDIENTS
225g/8oz prepared puff pastry
2-3 tbsps damson or plum jam
60g/2oz almond paste or
  marzipan, coarsely grated
120g/4oz butter
120g/4oz caster sugar
2 eggs, size 3, beaten
120g/4oz self-raising flour, sieved
2-3 tbsps milk
½ tsp almond essence

Preheat an oven to 200°C/400°F/ Gas Mark 6. Roll out two-thirds of the pastry and use it to line a 20cm/8-inch spring-form tin. Roll out the remaining pastry and cut it into strips to be used for lattice over the filling of the tart – do this now, so that the tart may be baked as quickly as possible once the filling is completed. Spread the jam over the base of the pastry, then scatter it with the grated almond paste.

Cream the butter and sugar together until light and fluffy, then gradually add the beaten eggs. Add 1 tablespoon of the flour before adding the second egg. Add the milk and almond essence, then fold in the remaining flour. Spoon the sponge mixture over the jam and almond paste, then arrange the pastry strips over the filling in a lattice pattern. Bake for 20 minutes, then reduce the oven temperature to 180°C/350°F/Gas Mark 4 and bake for a further 15 minutes, until the filling is browned and set. Serve warm with custard or cream.

EVERLASTING SYLLABUB

Syllabub was originally a mixture made by mixing milk, straight from the cow, with ale or wine to produce a foamy, frothy drink. It is a rather more luxurious mixture now.

Serves 4

INGREDIENTS
150ml/¼ pint dry white wine
2 tbsps brandy
Grated rind and juice of 1 lemon
60g/2oz caster sugar
280ml/½ pint double cream
Freshly grated nutmeg

Stir the wine, brandy, lemon rind and juice together and leave to stand for at least 2 hours. Add the caster sugar and stir until dissolved.

Whisk the cream until it begins to thicken, then gradually add the wine mixture and continue whisking until the mixture stands in soft peaks. Spoon into individual glasses and grate a little nutmeg on top. Chill before serving.

QUEEN OF PUDDINGS

This is one of my very favourite puddings – I like it warm or cold, and I sometimes use lemon curd between the base and the meringue instead of the more traditional red jam.

Serves 4-6

INGREDIENTS
430ml/¾ pint milk
30g/1oz butter
120g/4oz fresh white
   breadcrumbs
90g/3oz caster sugar
Grated rind of 1 lemon
2 eggs, size 3, separated
2 tbsps seedless red jam

Preheat an oven to 180°C/350°F/ Gas Mark 4. Heat the milk with the butter until the butter has melted, then add it to the breadcrumbs with half the sugar and the lemon rind; leave to stand for 10-15 minutes. Beat in the egg yolks, then pour the mixture into a buttered pie dish and bake for about 25 minutes, until just set.

Carefully spread the jam over the custard base – warm it, if necessary, to make it softer and therefore easier to spread. Whisk the egg whites until stiff, then gradually whisk in the remaining sugar. Pile the meringue into the dish, covering the base completely and forking it up into soft peaks. Bake for a further 10-15 minutes, until the meringue is lightly golden. Serve warm or cold.

RASPBERRY SOUFFLÉ

*Irish gardens produce marvellous crops of raspberries
because of the relatively mild climate. This is a popular way
of using the fruit towards the middle of the season – when
they first arrive they are eaten simply with sugar and cream.*

Serves 6

INGREDIENTS
460g/1lb raspberries
60g/2oz icing sugar, sieved
15g/½oz gelatine
150ml/¼ pint hot water
4 eggs, size 3, separated
120g/4oz caster sugar
280ml/½ pint whipping cream
Sprigs of mint or chopped
   hazelnuts to decorate

Tie a double thickness of baking
parchment around a 15cm/6-inch
soufflé dish to form a collar above
the rim of the dish. Reserve 4 or 5
raspberries for garnish, then sieve
the rest to remove the pips; stir
the icing sugar into the resulting
purée.

Scatter the gelatine over the hot
water and stir well; leave to stand
for 2-3 minutes to allow the
gelatine to dissolve. Heat gently
over a pan of water if necessary to
finish dissolving the granules, but
do not allow the mixture to boil.
Whisk the egg yolks and caster
sugar together over a pan of hot
water until thick and pale in
colour, then remove the bowl
from the heat and stir in the
raspberry purée followed by the
gelatine mixture. Whisk the cream
until thick and floppy but not stiff,
then fold half of it into the
raspberry base. Whisk the egg
whites until stiff, then fold them
into the mixture and spoon into
the prepared dish.

Chill for 2-3 hours, until set, then
remove the paper collar and
decorate with the remaining
whipped cream, whipping it a
little more if necessary, the
reserved raspberries and sprigs of
mint or chopped hazelnuts.

SUMMER PUDDING

As a nation of bakers, the Irish have a distinct advantage when it comes to making this classic summer dessert. The secret of a successful summer pudding is to use good home-made bread – commercial sliced bread becomes slimy and unpalatable.

Serves 8

INGREDIENTS
900g/2lbs soft fruits in season:
  redcurrants, blackcurrants,
  raspberries, blackberries etc.
120g/4oz sugar, or to taste
3-4 tbsps water
8-10 thin slices good white bread,
  crusts removed
Whipped cream for serving

Pick over the fruits, topping and tailing them as necessary, then place them in a pan with the sugar and water. Cook slowly for about 10 minutes, until the fruits are just starting to burst, then allow them to cool.

Cut the slices of bread to line an 850ml/1½-pint pudding basin. Dip them into the juices from the fruit then place them in the bowl, ensuring that it is fully lined, with no gaps. Pile the fruit into the bowl, then cover the pudding with the remaining bread, pressing it into the juices and turning it over so that the coloured side is uppermost. Cover the bowl with a side plate or breakfast plate and place a heavy weight on top.

Chill the pudding for at least 4 hours – overnight is best. Turn out onto a plate and serve sliced with cream.

IRISH PANCAKES

The Irish traditionally serve their pancakes rather thick.
They make the batter with buttermilk and serve the finished
pancakes in a stack with butter and sugar trickling down
the sides.

Serves 4

INGREDIENTS
225g/8oz flour
1 tsp salt
1 tsp bicarbonate of soda
2 eggs, size 3, beaten
280ml/½ pint buttermilk, approx
Butter and sugar for serving

Sieve the flour, salt and
bicarbonate of soda together into
a bowl and make a well in the
centre. Add the eggs and then the
buttermilk, a little at a time, to
give a thick batter.

Heat a heavy-based frying-pan
until hot, then butter it lightly and
cook spoonfuls of the mixture
quickly on both sides until golden
brown. Butter the pancakes as
soon as they are cooked and
sprinkle them with caster or
demerara sugar. Stack them on an
ovenproof plate and keep them
warm until all the batter has been
cooked.

SPICED CHEESECAKES

Cheesecakes have been a popular dessert for many centuries – not the thick creamy gateaux with fruit toppings which we are so familiar with now, but individual pastry tartlets with a dry, cloying filling.

Makes 12

INGREDIENTS
150ml/¼ pint milk
90g/3oz fresh white breadcrumbs
120g/4oz flour
Pinch of salt
60g/2oz butter
Cold water to mix
2 eggs, size 3, separated
30g/1oz butter
90g/3oz caster sugar
Good pinch ground nutmeg
Good pinch ground cinnamon
45g/1½oz currants

Bring the milk almost to the boil, then pour it over the breadcrumbs and leave for 15 minutes.

Preheat an oven to 220°C/425°F/ Gas Mark 7. Sieve the flour and salt into a bowl, then rub in the butter until the mixture resembles fine breadcrumbs. Mix to a manageable dough with cold water, then roll out and use to line a tray of patty tins. Prick the bases lightly with a fork.

Cream the butter until soft, then beat in the cooled breadcrumb mixture. Stir in the sugar and the spices, then add the currants and mix well. Add the egg yolks, then stiffly whisk the whites and finally fold them into the mixture.

Bake for 15-20 minutes until lightly browned and set.

BAKED EGG CUSTARD

*This is one of my favourite desserts and it is so easy to make.
Once the custard is baking I suggest cooking some fresh
fruits – plums, damsons or apples – with sugar and a little
water in the oven at the same time. I like my custard to set
firm so I always use four eggs; three eggs will produce a set,
albeit a little softer.*

Serves 4-5

INGREDIENTS
4 eggs, size 3, beaten
30g/1oz caster sugar
Vanilla essence
570ml/1 pint milk
Freshly grated nutmeg

Preheat an oven to 160°C/325°F/
Gas Mark 3 and lightly butter 4-5
ramekin dishes.

Beat the eggs with the sugar and
add a few drops of vanilla essence.
Heat the milk until almost boiling,
then pour it slowly onto the egg

mixture, whisking all the time.
Strain the custard through a sieve
into the prepared ramekin dishes
and grate a little fresh nutmeg
over each custard.

Place the filled ramekins in a
roasting tin, then fill the roasting
tin with boiling water, to come
about half way up the sides of the
dishes. Bake the custards in the
oven for 45 minutes, until just set.
Serve warm or cold.

RHUBARB LEMON PIE

Rhubarb is a popular fruit to grow in Ireland – it often grows well under the same conditions as potatoes. The first of the season's crop, while the stalks are small and the colour a vibrant pink, should simply be stewed and savoured. As the crop progresses, more adventurous ideas for using the rhubarb can be tried.

Serves 4-6

INGREDIENTS
175g/6oz flour
Pinch of salt
90g/3oz butter, cut into small
   pieces
680g/1½lbs rhubarb, trimmed and
   sliced
175g/6oz caster sugar
1 tbsp flour
1 egg, size 3, beaten
1 lemon, grated rind and juice
3 tbsps water

Preheat an oven to 220°C/425°F/ Gas Mark 7. Sieve the flour and salt into a bowl, then rub in the butter until the mixture resembles fine breadcrumbs. Mix to a firm but manageable dough, then roll out and use to line a 20cm/8-inch flan dish or sandwich tin. Fill the pastry shell with the prepared rhubarb.

Combine the sugar with the tablespoon of flour in a bowl, then add the egg and the remaining ingredients. Place the bowl over a pan of hot water and whisk until pale and slightly thickened. Pour the mixture over the rhubarb, then decorate with pastry leaves made from any pastry trimmings.

Bake the pie for 40 minutes, until set. Serve warm or cold.

PLUM STRUDEL FLAN

I think that plums are a much under-rated fruit and I enjoy puddings such as this, made with fresh fruits, in the early autumn.

Serves 6

INGREDIENTS
175g/6oz plain flour
Pinch of salt
150g/5oz butter, cut into small
  pieces
340g/12oz dessert plums, halved
  and stones removed
120g/4oz caster sugar
¼ tsp ground nutmeg
1 egg, size 3, beaten
90g/3oz flour
120g/4oz soft brown sugar

Preheat an oven to 200°C/400°F/ Gas Mark 6. Sieve the flour and salt into a bowl then rub in 90g/3oz of the butter, until the mixture resembles fine breadcrumbs. Mix to a firm, manageable dough with cold water, then roll out the pastry and use to line a 20cm/8-inch sandwich tin or flan dish.

Arrange the plums in the pastry case and sprinkle them with the caster sugar and nutmeg, then pour the beaten egg over the fruit.

Rub the remaining butter into the flour until the mixture resembles fine breadcrumbs, then stir in the brown sugar. Spoon the crumbs over the plums, then bake the flan for 40 minutes, until the topping is set and browned. Serve hot with cream or custard.

FRESH FRUIT PLUM PUDDING

This is a popular dish from Victorian times – doubtless a favourite at the first country house hunting parties of the season.

Serves 4-6

INGREDIENTS
340g/12oz self-raising flour
1 tbsp caster sugar
175g/6oz shredded suet
Cold water to mix
680g/1½lbs dessert plums, halved
  and stoned
120g/4oz soft brown sugar
1 tsp ground cinnamon, optional

Sieve the flour and salt into a bowl, then add the suet and sufficient cold water to make a soft but manageable dough. Turn out onto a lightly floured surface and knead gently, then roll out two-thirds of the pastry and use it to line an 850ml/1½-pint pudding basin.

Pack the plums into the basin, layering them with the sugar –

add a little ground cinnamon if desired. Roll out the remaining suet crust pastry to form a lid for the pudding, damp the edges with cold water; cover the pudding and seal the pastry edges together. Make a small slit in the top to allow the steam to escape, then cover the basin with greased greaseproof paper and foil, tying it securely in place.

Steam the pudding on a trivet in a pan of water for 2 hours – cover the pan and top up the water from time to time to prevent the pudding from boiling dry.

Turn the cooked pudding out onto a large warmed plate and serve sliced with custard or egg custard sauce.

BREAD & BAKING

According to a friend of mine, it is second nature for the Irish to bake. It is not surprising to discover, therefore, that breads and cakes are among the most traditional of Irish foods. In times gone by, having bread on the table meant life itself; today this basic need remains deeply rooted in the Irish psyche and manifests itself in the special respect reserved for the 'staff of life'.

Bread from a Variety of Grains

Bread was traditionally baked from whatever grains were to hand. Wheat, of course, produces the most common flour today, but other grains, such as barley and rye, were more common and, if grains were in short supply, then dried peas and pulses were ground up to be used. Wheat flour was reserved for the rich. Barley bread was eaten by monks who often followed very rigorous diets – it was described as a 'woody bread of barley'. The most common bread was an oaten loaf made with a mixture of flour and oatmeal. During the great potato famine, cornmeal or maizemeal was introduced from America to help relieve the starvation. Whilst welcome at the time, cornmeal breads have never really become popular in Ireland and, despite being quick to mix and bake, have not in any way replaced soda breads.

Soda Bread – an Irish Speciality

Yeasted loaves have really only become popular and widely available during this century, which perhaps explains the great daily tradition of Irish baking. Even today, most people who bake daily bake soda bread, a mixture that is very similar to a scone dough and one that is easily spoilt by over-mixing or kneading. The bread is therefore very quick to make; the ingredients just have to be combined rather than mixed, and then transferred to a tin and baked immediately. Soda bread is best eaten on the day that it is baked, so I always make a small loaf that can virtually be eaten in one go.

Soda breads were easy to cook on griddles if they were rolled thinly and cut into farls, while loaves were cooked in a upturned pot over the ashes of the fire, often with hot turfs placed on top to create an oven. These ovens, known as bastaples, were still in common use at the turn of the century.

Buttermilk for Flavour

A vital ingredient in Irish bread is buttermilk. Traditionally a by-product of the butter-making process, it is now available as a cultured milk product in many supermarkets. The culture in the buttermilk helps the rising process, producing a light loaf with a great depth of flavour. A mixture of bread- or baking-soda, both alternative names for bicarbonate of soda, and buttermilk provides sufficient raising agent for breads made from cereals or flour mixed with potatoes or oats. In many country areas soda bread would have been made with home-made buttermilk after the butter-making had been finished.

Even today, many traditional Irish baked goods are not cooked in an oven but on a griddle or in a heavy-based frying-pan on the hob. Baking was carried out in this way for centuries before the oven was a common domestic installation. As a consequence, the art of griddle baking had been perfected by the Irish, who saw little reason to change their methods and techniques. Thus many traditional Irish breads are baked in an unusual way from unusual ingredients and they have a unique and delicious flavour.

Cakes were only baked for special occasions, at least until the oven became commonplace and baking was less of a hit and miss affair over the ashes of a dying fire. There is an old Irish superstition called 'nipping the cake', whereby a small piece was broken off a freshly baked cake to avert bad luck – it just sounds like a good excuse for a nibble to me!

Hospitality and Home Baking

The Irish are renowned for their hospitality and it is therefore no surprise to find that their baking skills now extend far beyond bread baking to cakes, pastries and biscuits. It is still almost impossible to escape without a cup of tea or coffee when calling on friends and there is usually a cake or biscuit, freshly baked, to be enjoyed with it. In country areas drop scones or griddle cakes were often served as a mid-morning snack and were not reserved solely for tea-time eating. A high tea of cakes and scones was an important meal at harvest time, when the labourers would work late into the evening to make the best of the light, before coming back from the fields to their main meal of the day. With the dairy industry in Ireland producing such rich butter and creamy milk, it is no surprise that Irish baking tastes so good.

In the recipes that follow, I have only referred to butter in the ingredients. Whilst I am addicted to it and cannot conceive of choosing an alternative for traditional baking in my kitchen, margarine may be used as a substitute.

IRISH SODA BREAD

The Irish are a nation of bakers and many still bake their bread daily. The traditional bread is soda bread, the ingredients for which require no kneading – they are simply mixed and baked. This is an authentic recipe – white flour was for many years far more expensive than wholewheat. Once baked, soda bread would be wrapped in a damp cloth and stored on its side in a basket.

Makes 1 large loaf

INGREDIENTS
225g/8oz plain flour
1 tsp salt
1 tsp sugar
1 tsp bicarbonate of soda
1 tsp cream of tartar
460g/1lb wholewheat flour
460ml/16 fl oz buttermilk, sour milk or fresh milk with 1 tbsp yogurt
Milk for glazing

Preheat an oven to 200°C/400°F/Gas Mark 6. Sieve the flour, salt, sugar, bicarbonate of soda and cream of tartar into a bowl and stir in the wholewheat flour – use heaped teaspoon measures of the raising agents.

Make a well in the centre, pour in the buttermilk and mix quickly with a palette knife until the mixture forms a rough ball.

Shape into a round on a lightly floured surface – do not knead or the soda bread will be heavy. Place on a floured baking sheet and score the top into four sections with a sharp knife, then brush the loaf with a little milk. Bake in the preheated oven for 40 minutes, or until the loaf sounds hollow when tapped. Cool before slicing and serving.

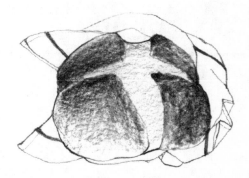

WHITE SULTANA
SODA BREAD

Sultanas add a touch of sweetness to this tasty teatime bread. All soda breads are made with ordinary plain flour as they do not rise like yeasted breads and are similar to a scone mixture.

Makes 1 loaf

INGREDIENTS
460g/1lb plain flour
1 tsp salt
1 tsp bicarbonate of soda
1 tsp cream of tartar
1 tbsp sugar
90g/3oz sultanas
280ml/½ pint buttermilk, sour milk or fresh milk with 1 tbsp yogurt

Preheat an oven to 200°C/400°F/ Gas Mark 6. Sieve the flour, salt, bicarbonate of soda and cream of tartar into a bowl, then stir in the sugar and sultanas. Make a well in the centre, pour in the buttermilk and mix quickly to a rough ball with a palette knife – do not over-mix. Shape lightly into a round on a floured surface, then bake the loaf on a floured baking sheet for 25-30 minutes, until the base sounds hollow when tapped. Cool before slicing and serving.

BARM BRACK

This is the traditional fruit bread of Ireland and is delicious served warm and buttered. In contemporary Irish cookery it is often toasted and served as a base for caramelised fruits. If made at Halloween the loaf traditionally has a ring hidden in it – the person who finds the charm is said to be the next to wed.

Makes 1 large loaf

INGREDIENTS
20g/¾oz fresh yeast
280ml/½ pint tepid milk
460g/1lb flour
½ tsp salt
½ tsp ground cinnamon
Pinch of grated nutmeg
60g/2oz butter
90g/3oz caster sugar
1 egg, size 2, beaten
225g/8oz sultanas
175g/6oz currants
60g/2oz chopped mixed peel

Glaze
1 tbsp sugar
4 tbsps water

Crumble the yeast into the tepid milk and leave for 2-3 minutes. Sieve the flour, salt and spices into a bowl, then rub in the butter and stir in the sugar. Stir the milk to ensure that the yeast has completely dissolved, then add it to the bowl with the beaten egg and mix the whole to a manageable dough.

Knead the dough thoroughly until it is smooth and elastic, then gradually work in the fruit. Shape the dough into one large loaf or halve it and place in two greased loaf tins or sandwich tins. Leave the barm brack to rise until doubled in size – this will take 1½-2 hours as it is a rich dough, heavy with fruit.

Preheat an oven to 200°C/400°F/ Gas Mark 6. Bake the breads for 45-60 minutes, or until the base sounds hollow when tapped. Dissolve the sugar for the glaze in the water and boil until reduced to a syrup. Brush the barm brack with the glaze as soon as it is cooked, then cool on a wire rack. Loaves baked in sandwich tins will require less time to cook than those baked in loaf tins.

IRISH BREACHED BREAD

This fruit loaf was served on special occasions, rather like a barm brack. Breached means speckled or spotted, which describes the appearance of the bread perfectly.

Makes 1 large loaf

INGREDIENTS
225g/8oz strong plain flour
60g/2oz butter
1 tsp easy-blend yeast
60g/2oz sugar
60g/2oz currants
60g/2oz raisins
30g/1oz flaked almonds
15g/½oz candied orange peel,
   chopped
225ml/8 fl oz warm water

Rub the butter into the flour, then stir in the yeast, the dried fruits and almonds. Add sufficient warm water to make a firm dough and knead thoroughly until smooth and elastic – the fruit may break up slightly, but this only adds to the speckled appearance of the bread.

Shape the dough into an oval loaf and place on a floured baking sheet; cover and leave in a warm place for about 1 hour, until almost doubled in size.

Preheat an oven to 200°C/400°F/ Gas Mark 6. Bake the loaf for 30-40 minutes, until golden brown – the base should sound hollow when the bread is cooked. Cool on a wire rack before serving sliced and buttered.

POTATO BREAD

This unusual bread follows a Victorian recipe and stays moist longer than many wheaten breads.

Makes 1 large loaf

INGREDIENTS
225g/8oz potatoes
340g/12oz strong white flour
120g/4oz flour
2 tsps easy-blend yeast
1 tsp salt
30g/1oz butter
225ml/8 fl oz warm water

Peel the potatoes and boil them until just tender. Drain and allow to cool slightly, then grate them coarsely.

Mix the flours with the yeast and salt; rub in the butter and add the grated potatoes. Mix to a manageable dough with the warm water, then turn onto a floured surface and knead thoroughly, until smooth and fairly elastic. Shape into a loaf and place in a greased 900g/2lb loaf tin. Cover with cling film or a damp tea towel and leave to rise in a warm place for 1 hour, until almost doubled in size.

Preheat an oven to 230°C/425°F/ Gas Mark 7. Bake the bread for 45 minutes, or until the base sounds hollow when tapped. Cool on a wire rack.

TREACLE BREAD

Treacle adds colour and a depth of flavour to breads – this loaf is lightly spiced with ginger and would traditionally be served sliced or cut into squares and sprinkled with sugar.

Makes 1 round loaf

INGREDIENTS
3 tbsps treacle
150ml/¼ pint milk
60g/2oz butter or margarine
60g/2oz soft brown sugar
225g/8oz self-raising flour
Pinch of baking powder
1 tbsp ground ginger
1 egg, size 3, beaten
30g/1oz caster sugar

Preheat an oven to 190°C/375°F/ Gas Mark 5 and lightly grease a 17.5-20cm/7-8-inch sandwich tin. Warm the treacle in the milk until the treacle has melted and the mixture is tepid. Cream the butter and brown sugar together until pale and fluffy, then add the treacle mixture. Sieve the flour, baking powder and ginger together and fold them into the mixture; add the egg and beat well.

Turn the mixture into the prepared tin and smooth the top. Bake for 1 hour, then cool the bread on a wire rack. Scatter the top of the treacle loaf with the caster sugar while it is still hot.

APRICOT NUT LOAF

This fruit loaf has a fresh, tangy flavour and is delicious
spread with butter and apricot jam.

Makes 1 loaf

INGREDIENTS
460g/1lb self-raising flour
Pinch of baking powder
¼ tsp salt
60g/2oz butter
60g/2oz sugar
Grated rind and juice of 1 orange
175g/6oz ready-to-eat dried
    apricots, finely chopped
30g/1oz walnuts, chopped
1 egg, size 3, beaten
430ml/¾ pint milk
1-2 tbsps orange juice

Preheat an oven to 180°C/350°F/
Gas Mark 4 and lightly grease a

900g/2lb loaf tin. Sieve the flour, baking powder and salt together into a bowl, then rub in the butter. Stir in the sugar, orange rind, apricots and walnuts. Beat the egg with the milk and mix with the flour to a stiff dropping consistency, adding as much orange juice as necessary.

Turn the mixture into the prepared tin and smooth the top of the loaf. Bake for 60-70 minutes, then allow to cool for a few minutes before turning out onto a cooling rack. Serve sliced and buttered.

GRIDDLE CAKES

Griddles were the first method of baking in many homes as they could be hung over a low fire and used for breads and scone mixtures. Griddle cakes, or drop scones, are probably the best known of griddle bakes and are very easy to make. Use a heavy frying pan if you do not have a griddle.

Makes about 18

INGREDIENTS
340g/12oz flour
1 tsp baking powder
½ tsp salt
30g/1oz caster sugar
2 eggs, size 3, beaten
430ml/¾ pint milk
60g/2oz butter, melted

Sieve the flour, baking powder and salt together into a bowl then stir in the sugar. Whisk the eggs with the milk and gradually beat them into the mixture to make a thick batter, then add the melted butter.

Preheat a griddle or heavy-based frying pan – test it by flicking a few drops of water at the surface which will splutter and 'dance' or roll when the pan is ready. Tip spoonfuls of mixture onto the griddle from the broad edge of a tablespoon. The griddle cakes are ready to turn when the bubbles rise and break on the surface of the mixture. Turn and cook the second side until lightly browned.

Keep the griddle cakes warm in a clean, folded tea-towel while cooking the rest of the mixture. Alternatively, any uncooked mixture may be stored covered in the fridge for 24 hours.

BOXTY PANCAKES

Boxty pancakes and breads are traditional in the northern counties of Ireland – they are made with a mixture of raw and mashed potatoes. When served with milk and salt they were called 'dippity'.

Serves 6

INGREDIENTS
225g/8oz peeled potatoes, grated
225g/8oz cooked mashed
  potatoes
225g/8oz flour
1 tsp bicarbonate of soda
1 tsp salt
Freshly ground black pepper
60g/2oz butter, melted
Milk
Oil for cooking

Squeeze the grated potato dry over a bowl, collecting the starchy water that is pressed out. Mix the grated potato with the mashed potato. Drain the water from the bowl and mix the remaining starchy deposits into the potato with the flour, bicarbonate of soda, salt and pepper. Stir in the butter and mix well, adding as much milk as necessary to give a batter of thick dropping consistency.

Heat a griddle or a heavy-based frying pan until water flicked onto it splutters into balls. Brush the griddle lightly with oil then cook spoonfuls of the mixture until browned and crispy on both sides.

POTATO CAKES

These are often served as part of a fried breakfast. Many supermarkets now sell them, but they are easy to make at home and so much nicer, too.

Serves 4

INGREDIENTS
90g/3oz flour
Pinch of salt
¼ tsp baking powder
20g/¾oz butter
340g/12oz cooked mashed potato
Oil or dripping for cooking

Sieve the flour, salt and baking powder together then rub in the butter. Stir in the mashed potato and knead the mixture into a ball. Roll out into a circle about 6mm/¼ inch thick and cut into 4 farls.

Heat a griddle or heavy-based frying-pan until hot then brush it with oil or dripping. Cook the farls for 2-3 minutes on each side, then serve with bacon and egg.

OATCAKES

Oatcakes are eaten with cheese, or spread with butter and thick honey. They are one of the most traditional of all Irish foods.

Makes 16

INGREDIENTS
120g/4oz flour
1 tsp salt
1 tsp baking powder
225g/8oz medium oatmeal
60ml/2 fl oz water
30g/1oz butter, lard or dripping

Sieve the flour, salt and baking powder into a bowl containing the oatmeal and mix well. Heat the water and fat together until the fat has melted, then pour the mixture into the dry ingredients and mix quickly together, adding a little extra water if necessary.

Divide the dough into two and roll out on a surface coated with oatmeal – the dough should be less than 6mm/¼ inch thick. Cut into 7.5cm/3-inch rounds, then cook the biscuits on a hot, lightly greased griddle or in a heavy-based frying pan until pale golden in colour. Leave the biscuits to cool and harden on a wire rack.

OATEN FARLS

There is a distinct Scottish influence in the cooking of the northern counties of Ireland and oatmeal is used extensively in local recipes. It gives a nutty flavour and texture to these potato farls. Use enough oatmeal when rolling out the farls to leave a good coating all over the cakes.

Serves 4

INGREDIENTS
90g/3oz flour
Pinch of salt
¼ tsp baking powder
20g/¾oz butter
340g/12oz cooked mashed potato
60g/2oz medium oatmeal
Oil or dripping for cooking

Sieve the flour, salt and baking powder together, then rub in the butter. Stir in the mashed potato and most of the oatmeal and knead into a ball. Roll out into a circle about 6mm/¼ inch thick using the remaining oatmeal to prevent the mixture from sticking to the work surface, then cut into 4 farls.

Heat a griddle or heavy-based frying pan until hot, then brush it with oil or dripping. Cook the farls for 2-3 minutes on each side and serve with bacon and egg.

CHRISTMAS GRIDDLE CAKES

These are a festive variation on the basic recipe for griddle cakes or drop scones – try them spread with a little brandy butter.

Makes about 18

INGREDIENTS
120g/4oz butter
120g/4oz caster or soft brown sugar
3 eggs, size 3, beaten
225g/8oz flour
1 tsp baking powder
Pinch of salt
Grated rind and juice of ½ lemon
120g/4oz currants

Cream the butter and sugar together until pale and fluffy, then gradually add the beaten eggs. Sieve the flour, baking powder and salt and add to the mixture with the lemon rind and juice and finally the currants – the mixture will be a thick, rich batter.

Heat a griddle or heavy-based frying pan until water flicked onto the surface splatters and forms into balls. Place tablespoonfuls of mixture on the griddle and cook until bubbles rise and break on the surface. Turn the griddle cakes over and cook until lightly browned on the second side. Keep the cooked griddle cakes warm in a clean dry tea towel while cooking the remaining mixture.

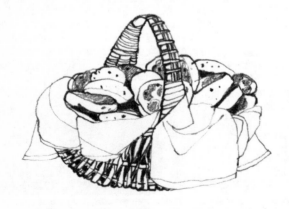

CHANKELE

*These fried cakes are also known as Christmas candles –
they are light in texture and very sweet.*

Makes 15-18

INGREDIENTS
Oil for deep-frying
3 eggs, size 3
150g/5oz icing sugar
175g/6oz ground almonds
120g/4oz flour
Sieved icing sugar

Preheat some oil in a deep-fryer
to about 190°C/375°F. Whisk the
eggs until light and pale in colour.
Add the sugar gradually, beating
with a wooden spoon until thick,
then stir in the ground almonds
and sufficient flour to make a soft
dough.

Turn the dough out onto a floured
surface and shape into thin rolls
resembling small candles. Fry the
cakes for 2-3 minutes, until
golden brown, then drain them
on crumpled absorbent kitchen
paper and dredge with sieved
icing sugar. Chankele are best
served hot.

POTATO APPLE

An autumn dish for eating round a bonfire. It would traditionally have been cooked on a griddle, but it is much easier to handle if cooked in the oven.

Serves 4

INGREDIENTS
460g/1lb freshly cooked mashed
  potatoes
60g/2oz butter
1 tsp ground ginger
60g/2oz demerara sugar
60g/2 oz flour
680g/1½lbs cooking apples,
  peeled, cored and sliced
Milk

15g/½oz butter
1 tbsp demerara sugar

Preheat an oven to 190°C/375°F/ Gas Mark 5. Mash the potatoes with the butter, ginger and 1 tbsp of the sugar, then add sufficient flour to make a workable dough. Divide into two and roll out into circles of about 17.5cm/7 inches – one should be slightly larger than the other.

Place the larger circle on a greased baking sheet and cover it with the sliced apples and remaining demerara sugar. Dampen the edges of the potato dough, cover the apple with the remaining potato crust and seal the edges together.

Make a small hole in the top to allow the steam to escape, then glaze the crust with milk and bake for 35-40 minutes, until the crust is browned. Carefully widen the slit in the top of the potato apple cake and slip the extra butter and sugar in over the hot apple filling so that it will caramelise over the mixture. Serve immediately, but remember that the apple filling will be very hot.

APPLE CAKE

Apple cake is a very traditional Irish bake – it is sometimes made with a potato crust, but this is a more traditional cake mixture.

Makes 1 cake

INGREDIENTS
175g/6oz butter
175g/6oz caster sugar
3 eggs, size 3, beaten
175g/6oz self-raising flour
1 tsp ground cinnamon
2 tbsps milk
2-3 dessert apples, peeled, cored and sliced

Preheat an oven to 180°C/350°F/ Gas Mark 4 and line a tin approx. 17.5x20cm/11x8 inches with baking parchment.

Cream the butter and sugar together until light and fluffy, then gradually add the eggs – fold 1 tbsp of flour in after each egg.

Sieve the remaining flour and cinnamon together and fold into the mixture, then add sufficient milk to give a soft dropping consistency. Spread half the cake mixture in the bottom of the prepared tin, then cover with the apple slices and top with the remaining mixture. Bake for 15 minutes, then reduce the oven temperature to 160°C/325°F/Gas Mark 3 and cook for a further 30 minutes, until golden brown.

Serve warm with custard or cream, or allow to cool completely on a wire rack, cut into squares and serve.

CHOCOLATE POTATO CAKE

This is a most unusual recipe for a cake, but it is delicious and has a slightly sharp flavour.

Makes 1 cake

INGREDIENTS
280g/10oz flour
½ tsp ground cinnamon
2 tsps baking powder
½ tsp salt
225g/8oz butter
460g/1lb caster sugar
4 eggs, size 3, separated
1 tsp vanilla essence
200g/7oz bar chocolate, grated
5 tbsps ground almonds
175g/6oz cold mashed potato
150ml/¼ pint milk

Preheat an oven to 180°C/350°F/ Gas Mark 4 and line a 900g/2lb loaf tin with baking parchment.

Sieve together the flour, cinnamon, baking powder and salt. Cream the butter and sugar until pale and fluffy, then gradually add the egg yolks and vanilla essence. Add 8 tablespoons of the grated chocolate, the ground almonds, cold potato and finally the flour and milk. Beat thoroughly until smooth.

Whisk the egg whites until stiff, then fold them into the potato mixture and turn into the prepared tin, levelling the top with the back of a spoon. Bake for about 1½ hours, until a skewer inserted into the cake comes out clean. Cool slightly in the tin before turning onto a wire rack to cool completely. Scatter any remaining chocolate over the cake.

214

MUFFINS

Muffins are easily spoiled by heavy-handed mixing and over-baking – keep everything to a minimum for perfect results!

Makes 8

INGREDIENTS
225g/8oz self-raising flour
Pinch of baking powder
½ tsp salt
45g/1½oz caster sugar
2 eggs, size 3, beaten
60g/2oz butter, softened
90ml/3 fl oz milk

Preheat an oven to 220°C/425°F/ Gas Mark 7 and grease a tray of muffin tins. Sieve together the flour, baking powder, salt and sugar. Beat the eggs with the butter and milk, then pour the mixture into the dry ingredients. Stir quickly and lightly to form a batter, then pour the mixture into the prepared muffin tins – they should be about two-thirds full. Bake immediately for 15-20 minutes, until well risen and set, then remove the muffins carefully from the tins and serve warm.

FRAUGHAN MUFFINS

Fraughan is the Irish name for blueberries, which are now widely available in supermarkets and make wonderful fruit muffins for special occasions.

Makes 8

INGREDIENTS
225g/8oz self-raising flour
Pinch of baking powder
120g/4oz caster sugar
½ tsp salt
60g/2oz butter, softened
120g/4oz blueberries
1 egg, size 3
150ml/¼ pint milk

Preheat an oven to 200°C/400°F/ Gas Mark 6 and grease a tray of muffin tins. Sieve all the dry ingredients together into a bowl, then add the butter, cutting it in with a knife until just blended. Stir in the fruit and add the whole egg and the milk. Stir until just blended, then spoon the mixture into the tins – they should be two-thirds full – and bake for 20-25 minutes. Serve warm.

SCONES

The Irish indulge their baking tradition in a generous hospitality at the tea table. Scones are very popular as an alternative to their close relative, soda bread. This is a basic recipe – fruit, sugar or grated cheese may be added.

Makes about 12

INGREDIENTS
340g/12oz self-raising flour
½ tsp salt
45g/1½oz butter
150ml/¼ pint milk

Preheat an oven to 230°C/450°F/ Gas Mark 8. Sieve the flour and salt together and rub in the butter, then stir in the milk to give a soft but manageable dough. Knead lightly on a floured surface and roll out to a circle 1.25cm/½-inch thick.

Cut the scones into 12 rounds using a fluted cutter and place on a floured baking sheet. Bake for 10-12 minutes, then cool on a wire rack.

BUTTERMILK SCONES

Buttermilk is used extensively in Irish baking and adds a great depth of flavour to otherwise bland mixtures.

Makes 15-18

INGREDIENTS
460g/1lb self-raising flour
½ tsp salt
90g/3oz butter
1 egg, size 3, beaten
175ml/6 fl oz buttermilk

Preheat an oven to 230°C/450°F/ Gas Mark 8. Sieve the dry ingredients together into a bowl, then rub in the butter. Beat the egg with the buttermilk and use the mixture to bind the scone dough together – add a little more buttermilk or milk if necessary.

Knead lightly, roll out on a floured surface until 1.25cm/½-inch thick and cut into rounds using a fluted cutter. Place the scones on a floured baking sheet and bake for 12-15 minutes. Cool on a wire rack.

SHORTBREAD

Irish traditions are very similar to those of the Scots and, especially in the northern counties, there is a great deal of Scottish influence in traditional dishes. It is not surprising, therefore, that the Irish have a great weakness for shortbread, which is often eaten at Christmas.

Serves 6-8

INGREDIENTS
120g/4oz flour
60g/2oz rice flour
60g/2oz caster sugar
120g/4oz butter
Caster sugar for dredging

Preheat an oven to 180°C/350°F/ Gas Mark 4 and lightly butter a 17.5cm/7-inch sandwich tin.

Mix the flours together in a bowl – use 175g/6oz plain flour if preferred and omit the rice flour – and stir in the sugar, then rub in the butter. Bring the dough together with your hand, press it into the prepared tin and smooth the surface with a palette knife. Mark into wedges and prick all over with a fork – I usually press a fork around the edge of my shortbread to give an attractively ridged crust to the biscuits.

Bake for 40-45 minutes, until pale golden, then score again as soon as the shortbread is removed from the oven. Dredge with caster sugar and break or cut when cold.

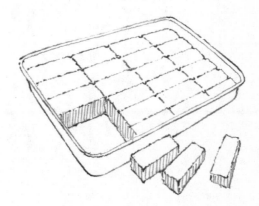

CARAWAY BISCUITS

Caraway seeds have become less popular as a spice for baked goods as other flavourings have become more widely available – I also think that a generation brought up on seed cake has tried hard to put the rest of us off this traditional flavouring. I like caraway in biscuits, where the flavour complements the butteriness of the dough.

Makes about 18

INGREDIENTS
120g/4oz butter
340g/12oz flour
120g/4oz caster sugar
½ tsp caraway seeds

Preheat an oven to 190°C/375°F/ Gas Mark 5 and lightly butter 2 baking sheets. Rub the butter into the flour until the mixture resembles fine breadcrumbs, then stir in the sugar and caraway seeds. Mix to a stiff dough with

2-3 tablespoons of cold water, knead lightly and roll out on a floured work surface until 6mm/¼ inch thick.

Cut into rounds using a floured cutter and place the biscuits on a baking sheet. Prick them with a fork and bake for 15 minutes. Allow the biscuits to harden slightly, then transfer to a wire rack to cool completely.

MACAROONS

Macaroons were a great favourite with the Victorians. This recipe will make them popular with your family and friends.

Makes about 24

INGREDIENTS

3 egg whites, size 3
225g/8oz ground almonds
225g/8oz caster sugar
Rice paper
Split almonds for decoration

Preheat an oven to 160°C/325°F/ Gas Mark 3 and line 2 baking sheets with rice paper.

Whisk the egg whites until stiff, then gradually fold in the ground almonds and sugar. Place teaspoonfuls of mixture on the rice paper, allowing plenty of room for the macaroons to spread, and place a piece of almond on each one.

Bake for about 20 minutes, until just beginning to colour. Tear any excess rice paper away from the sides of the macaroons then leave them to cool completely on wire racks.

GUINNESS CAKE

I like to keep this cake for a week before serving, and pour more Guinness into it after cooling – wrap the cake in foil while it is maturing.

Makes 1 large cake

INGREDIENTS
225g/8oz butter
225g/8oz soft brown sugar
280ml/½ pint Guinness
225g/8oz raisins
225g/8oz currants
225g/8oz sultanas
120g/4oz chopped mixed peel
570g/1¼lbs flour
½ tsp bicarbonate of soda
1 tsp mixed spice
1 tsp ground nutmeg
3 eggs, size 3, beaten
150ml/¼ pint extra Guinness

Place the butter, sugar and Guinness in a saucepan and bring slowly to the boil, stirring until the butter has melted and the sugar dissolved. Add the dried fruits and peel, and return the mixture to the boil. Simmer for 5 minutes, then leave until cold – the fruit will plump up in the liquid.

Preheat an oven to 160°C/325°F/ Gas Mark 3 then butter and line a 22.5cm/9-inch deep cake tin. Sieve the flour, bicarbonate of soda and spices into a large mixing bowl, stir in the cooled fruit mixture and add the beaten eggs. Beat well then turn into the prepared tin. Bake for 2 hours, until a skewer inserted into the cake comes out clean. Cool in the tin for 30 minutes before turning out onto a wire rack.

Make holes in the base of the cake and pour 4-5 spoonfuls of Guinness into the cake. Wrap it in foil and repeat this process daily for 3-4 days.

HONEY CAKE

Honey makes this cake very moist and also helps it to keep well.

Makes 1 large cake

INGREDIENTS
225g/8oz flour
Pinch of salt
¼ tsp grated nutmeg
¼ tsp ground cloves
½ tsp bicarbonate of soda
1 tsp cream of tartar
90g/3oz butter
120g/4oz raisins
60g/2oz chopped mixed peel
2 tbsps clear honey
2 eggs, size 3, beaten
3 tbsps milk

Preheat an oven to 200°C/400°F/ Gas Mark 6 and line a 900g/2lb loaf tin with baking parchment.

Sieve together the flour, salt, spices and raising agents, then rub in the butter and stir in the fruit. Beat the honey with the eggs, then add with sufficient milk to give a soft dropping consistency. Turn into the prepared tin and bake for 1¼-1½ hours. Cool briefly in the tin before turning out onto a wire rack.

SIMNEL CAKE

Although usually associated with Easter, simnel cakes were traditionally made for Mothering Sunday, the middle Sunday of Lent. The mixture was so rich that the cake lasted until Easter in the days when Lenten fasting was strictly observed.

Makes 1 large cake

INGREDIENTS
225g/8oz flour
½ tsp grated nutmeg
½ tsp ground cinnamon
½ tsp ground ginger
¼ tsp salt
1 tsp baking powder
225g/8oz butter
225g/8oz caster sugar
4 eggs, size 3, beaten
1 tsp vanilla essence
340g/12oz sultanas
340g/12oz currants
120g/4oz glacé cherries, halved
120g/4oz chopped mixed peel
1 tbsp milk
225g/8oz prepared almond paste

Preheat an oven to 160°C/325°F/ Gas Mark 3 and butter and double line a 22.5cm/9-inch deep cake tin with greaseproof paper or baking parchment.

Sieve the flour, spices, salt and baking powder together. Cream the butter and sugar until pale and fluffy, then gradually beat in the eggs and vanilla essence. Fold in the flour mixture and the prepared fruits alternately, then add sufficient milk to give a soft dropping consistency.

Place just over half the mixture in the prepared tin. Roll the almond paste into a 20cm/8-inch circle and place in the tin then spoon the remaining mixture over and smooth the top. Bake in the preheated oven for 3½-4 hours, until a skewer inserted into the cake comes out clean.

Allow the cake to cool slightly in the tin before removing it to a wire rack to cool completely. The top of the cake may be iced or decorated with more marzipan, brushed with apricot glaze and lightly browned under a hot grill.

POUND CAKE

This traditional cake is made with equal weights of flour, fat, sugar and eggs. I think it should really be called '10oz cake'.

Makes 1 cake

INGREDIENTS
280g/10oz butter
280g/10oz caster sugar
½ tsp vanilla essence
5 eggs, size 3, beaten
280g/10oz self-raising flour

Preheat an oven to 180°C/350°F/ Gas Mark 4 and line a 900g/2lb loaf tin with greaseproof paper or baking parchment.

Beat the butter, sugar and vanilla essence together, then gradually add the beaten eggs and fold in the flour. Spoon the mixture into the prepared tin and bake for 45 minutes, until a skewer inserted into the cake comes out clean. Cool the cake on a wire rack and serve sliced.

OLD-FASHIONED GINGERBREAD

This gingerbread is made with buttermilk, which gives a great depth of flavour to the cake – it should ideally be kept for 2-3 days before being served.

Makes 1 large cake

INGREDIENTS
340g/12oz flour
1 tsp cinnamon
1 tsp ground ginger
1 tsp bicarbonate of soda
¼ tsp salt
120g/4oz soft brown sugar
120g/4oz butter
2 eggs, size 3, beaten
6 tbsps treacle
280ml/½ pint buttermilk

Preheat an oven to 190°C/375°F/ Gas Mark 3 and line a 22.5cm/9-inch round sandwich tin with greaseproof paper or baking parchment.

Sieve the flour, spices, bicarbonate of soda and salt together and add the sugar. Melt the butter and stir the remaining ingredients into it before adding the mixture to the dry ingredients. Beat well, then turn into the prepared tin and bake for 1 hour, until a skewer inserted into the gingerbread comes out clean.

Cool on a wire rack, then cut into slices to serve.

BUTTERMILK SPICE CAKE

Spice cake is very popular in Ireland – the buttermilk gives the flavour an extra bite.

Makes 1 large cake

INGREDIENTS
340g/12oz self-raising flour
½ tsp baking powder
¼ tsp salt
½ tsp ground cloves
½ tsp ground cinnamon
90g/3oz caster sugar
60g/2oz soft brown sugar
90g/3oz butter, melted
280ml/½ pint buttermilk
2 eggs, size 3, beaten

Preheat an oven to 180°C/350°F/ Gas Mark 4 and line a 900g/2lb loaf tin with baking parchment.

Sieve the flour, baking powder, salt and spices together; stir in the sugars and make a well in the centre. Add the melted butter, buttermilk and beaten eggs, then beat thoroughly to a smooth batter – beat for 3-4 minutes to remove any lumps. Turn into the prepared tin and bake for 50-60 minutes. Cool on a wire rack and served sliced with butter.

ECONOMY SPICE CAKE

Boiled fruit cakes keep well and are always moist. They are also economical to make, especially when they do not contain eggs.

Makes 1 large cake

INGREDIENTS

280ml/½ pint water
340g/12oz sultanas
225g/8oz soft brown sugar
120g/4oz butter
340g/12oz flour
1 tsp baking powder
1 tsp bicarbonate of soda
1 tsp salt
½ tsp ground cinnamon
½ tsp ground allspice
Pinch of ground nutmeg
120g/4oz chopped mixed peel

Preheat an oven to 160°C/325°F/ Gas Mark 3 and lightly butter a 900g/2lb loaf tin. Heat the water, sultanas, sugar and butter together until the butter has melted; boil for 3 minutes. Cool slightly, then beat in the sieved dry ingredients and add the mixed peel.

Turn the mixture into the prepared tin and level the top, then bake for about 1½ hours, until a skewer inserted into the mixture comes out clean. Remove the cake from the tin and cool on a wire rack.

ROCK CAKES

*These are one of my favourite tea-time cakes – economical,
easy to make and so delicious when made with top
quality fruit.*

Makes 18

INGREDIENTS
225g/8oz self-raising flour
½ tsp salt
1 tsp mixed spice
90g/3oz butter
90g/3oz demerara sugar
1 egg, size 3, beaten
2-3 tbsps milk
Caster sugar for dredging

Preheat an oven to 200°C/400°F/
Gas Mark 6 and lightly butter 2
trays of patty tins or 2 baking
sheets. Sieve the flour, salt and
spices into a bowl and rub in the
butter. Stir the sugar into the
mixture, then add the egg and
sufficient milk to give a stiff
mixture.

Place spoonfuls of the mixture in
the patty tins or in piles on the
baking sheet and bake the rock
cakes for 12-15 minutes, until
golden brown. Transfer to a wire
cooling rack and dredge with
caster sugar while still hot.

VICTORIA SANDWICH CAKE

This cake was first served at royal tea parties during the reign of Queen Victoria, but it soon became a favourite throughout the land.

Makes 1 cake

INGREDIENTS
120g/4oz butter
120g/4oz caster sugar
2 eggs, size 3, beaten
Vanilla essence
120g/4oz self-raising flour, sieved
Raspberry jam
Sieved icing sugar

Preheat an oven to 180°C/350°F/ Gas Mark 4 and lightly butter two 17.5cm/7-inch sandwich tins.

Cream the butter and sugar together until pale and fluffy, then gradually add the beaten eggs and a few drops of vanilla essence. Fold in the sieved flour, then add 1-2 tbsps water, if necessary, to give a soft dropping consistency.

Divide the mixture equally between the two tins, then bake for about 25 minutes, until golden brown. The top of the sponges should spring back when lightly pressed if cooked.

Cool on a wire rack, then sandwich the cakes together with jam and sieve a little icing sugar over the top before serving.

CHERRY MADEIRA

Madeira cake should always be accompanied by a glass of Madeira wine, a very fashionable refreshment in Victorian times. A good Madeira cake will always crack on the top.

Makes 1 cake

INGREDIENTS
460g/1lb flour
30g/1oz cornflour
¼ tsp salt
2 tsps baking powder
150g/5oz butter
225g/8oz caster sugar
3 eggs, size 3, beaten
1 tsp vanilla essence
150ml/¼ pint milk
225g/8oz glacé cherries, washed
   and halved

Preheat an oven to 180°C/350°F/ Gas Mark 4 and line a deep 17.5-20cm/7-8 inch tin with baking parchment.

Sieve the flour, cornflour, salt and baking powder together. Cream the butter and sugar until pale and fluffy, then gradually add the beaten eggs and vanilla essence – fold in a tablespoon of flour if the mixture begins to curdle. Fold in the remaining flour mixture alternating it with the milk, then add the cherries. Turn the mixture into the prepared cake tin and bake for 1 hour, until a skewer inserted into the centre of the cake comes out clean. Cool on a wire rack.

SOUR MILK SPICE CAKES

*Nothing was ever wasted in country houses – sour milk was
used in baking as it helps the rising of most mixtures and
also adds extra flavour to scones and cakes.*

Makes about 15

INGREDIENTS
120g/4 oz butter
120g/4oz soft brown sugar
225g/8oz self-raising flour
½ tsp ground cinnamon
¼ tsp ground cloves
Pinch of salt
1 tsp bicarbonate of soda
2 eggs, size 3, beaten
1 tsp vanilla essence
4 tbsps sour milk
120g/4oz currants

Preheat an oven to 190°C/375°F/
Gas Mark 5 and lightly grease 2
trays of patty tins or line them
with paper cases.

Cream the butter and sugar
together until pale and fluffy.
Sieve the flour, spices and raising
agents. Beat the eggs into the
butter, a little at a time, and add
the vanilla essence; fold in the
flour, alternating it with the milk.
Fold in the currants, then use the
mixture to fill the patty tins – use
a generous tablespoonful of
mixture in each one. Bake the
cakes for 20 minutes, then allow
them to cool on a wire rack.

The spice cakes may be served
plain, or iced and decorated with
almonds or crystallised ginger.

YELLOWMAN

This toffee has been associated for centuries with the 'Ould Lammas Fair', which takes place every year at Ballycastle, Co. Antrim. It has been made by the same family for several hundred years.

Makes about 680g/1½lbs

INGREDIENTS
460g/1lb golden syrup
225g/8oz soft brown sugar
1 tablespoon softened butter
1 tsp baking powder
2 tbsps vinegar

Thoroughly butter a 15-17.5cm/6-7-inch square cake tin. Melt the butter in a large pan and coat the insides of the pan with it. Add the syrup, sugar and finally the vinegar and stir over a low heat until the sugar and syrup have dissolved. Bring to the boil, then simmer without stirring – test to see if the toffee is at setting point by dropping a little of the mixture into a cup of cold water – if it sets it is ready.

Add the baking powder carefully – it will make the mixture foam. Stir with a long-handled wooden spoon then pour the toffee into the prepared tin and mark into squares. Break into squares when completely cold.

The toffee was traditionally turned onto a slab and kneaded or pulled until pale yellow in colour, once it had cooled enough to handle. It was then chipped into pieces for sale and this is still the way it is sold at the Lammas Fair.

PRESERVES

It is one of the delightful vagaries of nature that many food crops are only available seasonally, with a glut of a specific fruits or vegetables available for short periods only. Before the advent of refrigerated storage and transportation, salting, pickling, curing and drying were common methods of preparing foods in times of plenty for use during lean months. The meat from a slaughtered animal could be cured for later use, fish would be salted and fruit preserved to ensure adequate supplies for year-round use. Today, home preserving is rarely a necessity, but it gives us access to a delightful range of taste sensations.

Bog Butter

Long-known for its medicinal properties, one of the most widely used of preservatives of former times was garlic. For centuries this was added to butter, which would then be placed in a casket and immersed in the cold waters of a bog until required. Some long-forgotten bog butter has been found in Ireland and traced back to the 6th century.

Jams and Jellies for Tea

With such a rich tradition of baking, an Irish high tea is an experience not to be missed – scones, griddle cakes, apple pie and shortbreads, followed by fruit cake and, of course, plenty of tea. Tea was first introduced to Ireland in the 18th century and was a drink of the wealthy and leisured classes. To a certain extent it was scorned by the rest of the population, who believed that it encouraged idleness and sloth. However, the beverage wasn't always a resounding success on first tasting – it is reported that some sailors' wives, when first presented with tea by their travelling husbands, boiled it up, threw away the liquor then offered the warm leaves to be eaten!

Many of the best jams are made from berry fruits, which grow abundantly in Ireland, being well suited to the mild, damp climate. In times gone by these were often used for making wine, then the discarded fruit would be boiled up and dried to make a fruit paste for eating through the winter. Although such preserves are still available, and are often favoured by mothers trying to prevent their children from eating too many sweets and chocolate bars, it is generally accepted that a better method of preserving fruits is to make them into jams and jellies, which can then be served with griddle cakes, scones and sponges, or used as fillings in pies and tarts.

Pickling Vegetables for Later Use

Many foods, including meat, have been pickled over the years – pickled pork was, until recently, a common Irish dish – but it is with vegetables that this method of preservation is most usually associated. Onions and beetroots are probably the most common vegetables to be pickled and it is easy to prepare them yourself at home. However, pickles do not last indefinitely and this is especially true of pickled onions, which should really be eaten within six months of being prepared as they will become soft.

Pickled cauliflower was a popular Irish relish in the 18th century; rather like a piccalilli without the mustard sauce it is rarely heard of today.

Mushrooms, cucumbers, walnuts and even eggs, although not traditional Irish pickle ingredients, would undoubtedly have been known because of their popularity in English households.

Testing your Jam for Setting

Many recipes for jams and jellies just end with words 'test for setting, then pot, seal and label'. The basic rules for jam making are very simple. Before starting to make your preserve, chill a plate in the fridge. As your jam boils you can then test for setting by spooning a little of the liquid onto the plate. Leave for 1-2 minutes, then drag your fingertip through the jam – if the surface wrinkles the jam will set. It is a good idea to draw the pan of jam off the heat while testing for setting so that it does not overcook. I find this method much easier and more reliable than relying on a sugar thermometer to check temperatures.

Jars for preserves should be clean and sterile before being filled – this helps to prevent a mould from forming on the food. Wash jars thoroughly in hot water, rinse and place in the oven at a low temperature to dry and to warm. If you have a dishwasher, run the jars through the regular wash cycle then place them straight into the oven to keep them warm.

Disks of waxed paper should be placed on the surface of the jam as soon as it has been poured into the pots to form a seal, then the pots should be covered, either with lids or with cellophane covers.

Always label your pots with the name of the preserve and the date that it was made. This ensures that they are eaten in rotation and not kept for too long.

STRAWBERRY JAM

Strawberry jam was a great favourite at the tea-table in Victorian times, just as it is today. The Victorians sometimes used redcurrant juice with the strawberries in place of lemon juice, allowing 280ml/½ pint per 460g/1lb fruit. Wexford is especially famous for its strawberries and there is a strawberry festival held there every year in July.

Makes about 4.1kg/9lbs

INGREDIENTS
2.7kg/6lbs ripe but firm
   strawberries
Juice of 2 lemons
2.7kg/6lbs granulated or
   preserving sugar

Hull the strawberries and rinse them briefly under cold water. Place the fruit in a preserving pan with the lemon juice and cook gently until the juices run from the fruit – do not overcook or the strawberries will break up.

Add the sugar and stir until it has completely dissolved, then simmer the jam gently for 30 minutes, stirring occasionally to prevent it from sticking. Remove any scum from the top of the jam and test for setting – the surface of the jam should wrinkle on a plate when pushed with a finger.

Pot the jam in clean, warm jars, then seal and label.

BLACKCURRANT JAM

*Blackcurrants are abundant in Ireland. They produce a
very thick, syrupy liquid and the jam must be stirred
frequently during cooking to prevent it from burning.*

Makes 3.6kg/8lbs

INGREDIENTS
1.8kg/4lbs blackcurrants, topped
   and tailed
1.7 litres/3 pints water
2.7kg/6lbs granulated or
   preserving sugar

Wash the blackcurrants and place
them in a preserving pan with the
water. Bring to the boil, then
simmer for about 30 minutes,
until the fruit is soft.

Add the sugar and stir off the heat
until it has completely dissolved.
Bring the jam to the boil and cook
rapidly until setting point is
reached. Pot in clean, warm jars,
then seal and label.

RASPBERRY JAM

*Providing that you do not overcook the fruit, your labours
will be rewarded with jam of a spectacular deep red colour
and a marvellous depth of flavour. The raspberries should
be very fresh – pick them yourself just before making the jam
if possible.*

Makes 2.7kg/6lbs

INGREDIENTS
1.8kg/4lbs raspberries
1.8kg/4lbs granulated or
   preserving sugar

Wash the raspberries, removing
any stalks, leaves or damaged
fruit. Place them in a pan and
cook gently until the fruit just
starts to burst, then remove the
pan from the heat and stir in the
sugar. Continue stirring until it
has completely dissolved.

Return the pan to the heat and
boil rapidly for 5 minutes, or until
setting point is reached. Pour the
jam into clean, warm jars, then
seal and label.

GREEN GOOSEBERRY JAM

This preserve may be rubbed through a sieve to remove the pips, and then used as a fruit purée in cakes and gateaux – I like it just as it is.

Makes 2.7kg/6lbs

INGREDIENTS
1.8kg/4lbs gooseberries
700ml/1¼ pints water
2.3kg/5lbs granulated or
   preserving sugar

Top and tail the gooseberries and wash them thoroughly, then place the fruit in a preserving pan with the water. Bring to the boil, then simmer for about 30 minutes, until the fruit is well softened.

Stir the sugar into the pan and continue stirring until it has completely dissolved. Boil the jam rapidly for 30 minutes, or until setting point is reached, stirring regularly to prevent the jam from sticking. Remove any scum from the top of the jam before pouring into clean, warm jars. Seal the jars then label.

APPLE BUTTER

This is an excellent preserve to make when there is a glut of apples – it is creamy in consistency with a slight caramel flavour.

Makes 900g/2lbs

INGREDIENTS
1.4kg/3lbs Bramley or Granny Smith's apples
150ml/¼ pint unsweetened apple juice
1 tsp ground cinnamon
Light brown sugar

Wash the apples and cut them into quarters but do not peel or core them. Place the fruit in a preserving pan with the apple juice and cinnamon and cook gently until soft and pulpy.

Push the softened apples through a sieve, discarding the cores, skins and pulp left behind. Weigh the apple pulp, return it to the rinsed out preserving pan and add 225g/8oz soft brown sugar for every 460g/1lb of pulp.

Stir the mixture over a low heat until the sugar has dissolved, then bring to the boil and simmer for 20-30 minutes, until the preserve is thick and creamy. Stir frequently to prevent the apple butter from sticking on the bottom of the pan.

Pour the preserve into clean, warmed jars then seal and label.

CRAB APPLE JELLY

*This is a traditional jelly to eat with pork or any cold meat.
Crab apples are popular trees in Irish gardens – you seldom
see the fruit in shops but if you have access to a tree, this is a
preserve that is well worth making.*

Makes about 1.8kg/4lbs

INGREDIENTS
1.8kg/4lbs crab apples
1.14 litres/2 pints water
Granulated sugar

Wash the crab apples and chop them roughly – there is no need to peel or core them. Place the fruit in a preserving pan, cover with the water and bring to the boil, then simmer for 30-40 minutes, until the fruit is very soft.

Pour the fruit into a jelly bag suspended over a bowl and leave for 3-4 hours, or overnight, until the bag stops dripping. Do not squeeze the bag or the jelly will become cloudy.

Measure the juice and return it to the preserving pan with 460g/1lb sugar for every 570ml/1 pint juice. Stir over a gentle heat until the sugar has dissolved, then bring to the boil and boil rapidly until setting point is reached. Remove any scum from the surface of the jelly, then pour into clean, warmed jars, seal and label.

REDCURRANT JELLY

Redcurrant jelly is seldom used as a jam and is mainly used in meat cookery, to serve with meat or to flavour sauces. It can be difficult to achieve a really good set with this jelly, but this is of no consequence if it is to be used as a seasoning.

Makes about 1.8kg/4lbs

INGREDIENTS
1.4kg/3lbs redcurrants
1.4kg/3lbs caster sugar

Top and tail the fruit, then wash the currants thoroughly. Mix them with the sugar in a preserving pan and bring the mixture rapidly to the boil. Remove any scum and continue cooking for 8-10 minutes.

Press the contents of the pan through a muslin-lined sieve to remove the remains of the currants, then pot the jelly in small, clean, warmed jars. Seal and label.

MINT & APPLE JELLY

Mint and apples are both plentiful in Ireland and this traditional preserve is particularly good served with roast lamb.

Makes 680g/1½lbs

INGREDIENTS

570ml/1 pint clear, unsweetened apple juice
1½ tbsps cider vinegar
570ml/1 pint water
Small bunch mint, chopped
680g/1½lbs preserving sugar with added pectin

Bring the apple juice, vinegar, water and half the mint to the boil in a preserving pan, then continue to cook rapidly for 5 minutes. Strain through a muslin-lined sieve, then return the liquid to the preserving pan, after rinsing it with cold water.

Stir the sugar into the pan and heat gently until it has dissolved. Bring to the boil, then boil rapidly for 5 minutes or until setting point is reached. Remove the pan from the heat and stir in the remaining mint, very finely chopped.

Pour the mint jelly into small, clean pots that have been warmed. Seal and label.

PRESERVED CHOPPED TOMATOES

This is an excellent way of keeping tomatoes for future use in sauces and stews – they have a much better flavour and colour than tomatoes which are frozen. This recipe produces a thick, well-flavoured purée.

Makes 2.3-2.7kg/5-6lbs

INGREDIENTS
2.3kg/5lbs firm, ripe tomatoes
2 large onions, finely chopped
150ml/¼ pint extra virgin olive oil
150ml/¼ pint white wine or herb
　vinegar
2 tbsps freshly chopped oregano
Salt and freshly ground black
　pepper
120g/4oz granulated sugar

Roughly chop the tomatoes, removing the cores, then place them in a preserving pan or large saucepan and cook slowly for 30-40 minutes, until softened to a pulp. Press the tomato mixture through a sieve to remove all skin and pips.

Cook the onions slowly in the oil until soft but not brown, then add them with all the remaining ingredients to the tomato pulp. Cook over a low heat for about 30 minutes, until the mixture has thickened and has a glossy appearance.

Pour into clean, warmed jars, then seal and label.

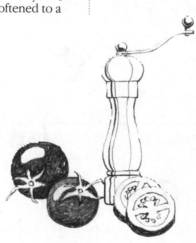

TOMATO SAUCE

I have to confess to a weakness for ready-made tomato sauce or ketchup. However, even that becomes second best to a home-made sauce. Tomatoes did not arrive in Ireland until the turn of the century, so this is a comparatively new recipe in the Irish kitchen.

Makes about 1.4kg/3lbs

INGREDIENTS
2.3kg/5lbs firm, ripe tomatoes
4 cloves garlic, roughly chopped
570ml/1 pint spiced vinegar
1 onion, finely chopped
Good pinch of salt
150ml/¼ pint soy sauce
150ml/¼ pint water
2-3 tbsps Worcestershire sauce

Wash the tomatoes and chop them roughly, then place them in a preserving pan or a large saucepan with the garlic, vinegar, onion and salt. Bring to the boil, then cook the mixture for about 20 minutes, until the onions and garlic have softened.

Press the tomato mixture through a sieve then return the purée to the rinsed out pan. Add the soy sauce, water and Worcestershire sauce and bring to the boil. Cook quickly for about 20 minutes, until the mixture has reduced slightly and thickened. Pour into clean, warmed jars and seal, then label. Keep the sauce for at least a week before using.

PICKLED ONIONS

There is nothing like a home-pickled onion! The perfect accompaniment to Crubeens, Dublin Coddle and so many other traditional recipes. Pickled onions do not keep for ever – they will become soft if not eaten within about 6 months of pickling.

Makes 1.4kg/3lbs

INGREDIENTS
1.4kg/3lbs pickling onions
340g/12oz salt
½ tsp allspice berries
½ tsp black peppercorns
850ml/1½ pints vinegar

Try to choose onions that are about the same size so that they pickle evenly. Place them, unpeeled, in a large bowl, then add half the salt in solution with sufficient water to cover them. Allow the onions to stand for 12 hours, then drain and peel them.

Make another brine solution with the remaining salt and sufficient water to cover the peeled onions, then leave them to soak for a further 24-36 hours, depending on the size of the onions. Remove the onions from the brine and pack them tightly into clean, warmed jars.

Add the spices to the vinegar and pour the mixture into the jars, ensuring that the onions are completely covered. Seal with metal lids to prevent the vinegar from evaporating, then label. Allow the onions to mature for 8 weeks before eating.

PICKLED BEETROOT

Beetroot have been popular in Ireland for hundreds of years and there are certainly records of them being pickled for the last two or three centuries. Indeed, one recipe from the mid-18th century suggests pickling them in a mixture of vinegar and claret – those were the days!

Makes 1.4kg/3lbs

INGREDIENTS
1.4kg/3lbs beetroot
1 tsp salt
15g/½oz black peppercorns
15g/½oz allspice berries
570ml/1 pint vinegar

Choose small, evenly-sized beetroots. Wash them carefully without breaking the skins to prevent 'bleeding' in the pan, then place them in a pan with the salt and cover with cold water. Bring slowly to the boil and simmer gently for about 2 hours, until tender. Remove the beetroots from the pan and leave them to cool.

Peel the beetroot, then cut into 1.25cm/½-inch slices or dice. Pack the pieces into clean, warmed jars. Boil the spices in the vinegar for 10 minutes, then allow the mixture to cool. Pour the cooled vinegar over the beetroot, ensuring that it is completely covered, then seal the jars with metal lids to prevent the vinegar from evaporating, and label.

MUSHROOM KETCHUP

Mushroom ketchup used to be eaten like gravy over boiled potatoes in Ireland – this must have given a very strong flavour and the ketchup is more often used now as a seasoning, by the teaspoonful. The best flavour is achieved by using flat, open mushrooms.

Makes about 570ml/1 pint

INGREDIENTS
1.8kg/4lbs flat, open mushrooms,
    roughly chopped
120g/4oz salt
Pinch of cayenne pepper
Pinch of ground allspice
Pinch of ground ginger
3 tbsps brandy

Layer the mushrooms with the salt in a glass bowl and leave for 3 days, stirring and mashing the mushrooms from time to time to encourage the juices to flow.

Strain the juices through a sieve into a pan and simmer for 15 minutes before adding the spices. Cook for a further 20 minutes, then remove the pan from the heat and allow the ketchup to cool completely. Add the brandy, then pour into clean, warmed bottles or jars and seal tightly, preferably with metal caps.

TARRAGON VINEGAR

This vinegar should be made in July or August, before the tarragon flowers, in order to get the very best flavour from the herb. It is particularly good for fish and chicken dishes.

Makes 1.14 litres/2 pints

INGREDIENTS
1 handful fresh tarragon
1.14 litres/2 pints white wine
  vinegar

Wash the tarragon, strip the leaves from any woody stalks but leave them on the softer stems from the tip of the plants. Bruise the leaves with the heel of a knife to allow the true flavour of the tarragon to escape into the vinegar.

Place the leaves in clean, warmed bottles, then pour the vinegar in over them. Cork or cover with metal lids and leave for at least 2 months.

If you intend to give the bottles of vinegar as gifts, strain the vinegar then pour it into fresh bottles. Add a few fresh sprigs of tarragon, then cork tightly and keep until required.

IRISH WHISKEY MUSTARD

Designer mustards are becoming just as popular in Ireland as they are elsewhere. It is easy and relatively cheap to make your own, and you can add as much whiskey as you like!

Makes about 460g/1lb

INGREDIENTS
175g/6oz yellow mustard seeds
60g/2oz black mustard seeds
60g/2oz sea salt
3 tbsps clear honey
90ml/3 fl oz white wine vinegar
60ml/2 fl oz whiskey

Soak the mustard seeds in hot water for 1 hour, then drain them in a sieve. Pat dry on absorbent kitchen paper, then crush the seeds roughly in a pestle and mortar. This may also be done in a food processor although I do not think this gives as good a flavour.

Transfer the seeds to a glass bowl and add the salt and honey, then stir in the vinegar and whiskey, beating well to ensure that all the ingredients, and especially the honey, are thoroughly mixed. Cover the bowl with a plate and leave the mustard overnight – it will thicken considerably during this standing period.

Taste the mustard and add any extra salt, honey or whiskey that is required. Pot the mustard in clean, warm jars and seal with metal lids. Label clearly and leave to mature for 2-3 weeks before using.

INDEX